Francis A. Schaeffer

the God who is there

Speaking
historic Christianity
into the
twentieth century

Inter-Varsity Press
Downers Grove
Illinois 60515

To the one
who has walked
hand in hand
with me
for a very short
thirty-five years

Acknowledgments

Thanks are due to the following for permission to quote from copyright works:

Madame Marguerite Arp for the poem '*für Theo van Doesburg*' by Hans Arp;

Dylan Thomas, *Collected Poems* © 1957 by New Directions Publishing Corporation. Reprinted by permission of New Directions Publishing Corporation;

the author and *The New Yorker* for an extract from 'Figure in an Imaginary Landscape' by Calvin Tomkins, © 1964 The New Yorker Magazine Inc.;

Agence Hoffman for an extract from the preface 'A Sense of Wonder' by Henry Miller to *The History of Art* by Elie Favre (in the translation which appeared in *Vogue*, December 1964);

Dr. John Macquarie for an extract from an article which appeared in *The Listener*, April 12, 1962.

Contents

SECTION I: *The intellectual and cultural climate of the second half of the twentieth century*

1. The Gulf is Fixed   13
   Before the chasm
   Presuppositional apologetics would have stopped the
     decay
   The line of despair
   Unity and disunity in rationalism
   Tendency towards a uniform culture

2. The First Step in the Line of Despair: Philosophy   20
   Hegel, the doorway
   Kierkegaard, the first man below
   The existentialism of Jaspers, Sartre, Heidegger
   The anti-philosophy of the Anglo-Saxon world
   The use of drugs
   What does and does not happen in these experiences

3. The Second Step: Art   30
   Van Gogh and Gauguin
   Cézanne and Picasso
   Mondrian
   Dada, Marcel Duchamp, the happenings and the
     environments

4. The Third and Fourth Steps: Music and the General Culture   37
   Musique concrète
   Henry Miller
   Philosophic homosexuality
   John Osborne
   Dylan Thomas
   Modern cinema, the mass media and the Beatles

5. The Unifying Factor in the Steps of Despair   44
   Romanticism is dead: Christianity's opportunity if
     antithesis is maintained

SECTION II: The Relationship of the New Theology to the Intellectual Climate

1. The Fifth Step: Theology   51
Departure from biblical Christianity

2. Modern Mysticism—Despair beyond Despair   55
Theology and semantic mysticism
The use of words and symbols
The origins of semantic mysticism—Leonardo da Vinci
Nature and Grace

3. Modern Mysticism in Action: Art and Language   63
The tension of being man
Mysticism in art—Klee and Dali
Mysticism in language—Heidegger

4. Modern Mysticism in Action: Music and Literature   70
Mysticism in music—Leonard Bernstein and John Cage
Mysticism in literature—Henry Miller

5. A New Phase of Modern Theology   78
God is dead—or almost so!
A quest by the upper storey men
Today's opportunity for the new theology

SECTION III: How Historic Christianity Differs from the New Theology

1. Personality or a Devilish Din   87
The logical end of denying personality

2. Verifiable Facts and Knowing   92
Divine and human communication
Love is more than a word

3. The Dilemma of Man   100
The scandal of the cross
Historic Christianity and man's dilemma

4. God's Answer to Man's Dilemma   105
There need be no either-or in *La Peste*

5. How do we Know it is True?   108
The nature of proof
True rationality but not only rationality
Who stands in the continuity of the Church?

SECTION IV: *Speaking Historic Christianity into the Twentieth Century Climate*

1. Finding the Point of Tension   119
   Communicating to one of my kind
   Logical conclusions
   Torn by two consistencies
   The tensions are felt in differing strengths

2. From the Point of Tension to the Gospel   126
   Why there is a place for conversation
   Giving and taking blows
   Taking the roof off

3. Applying the Gospel   131
   How dare we do it?
   Faith in the biblical sense

SECTION V: *Pre-Evangelism is no Soft Option*

1. Commending the Christian Faith to our Generation   139
   Defence of the faith
   Communication of the faith

2. The Importance of Truth   143
   Truth stands before conversion
   Truth and spirituality
   The God behind truth

SECTION VI: *Personal and Corporate Living into the Twentieth-Century Climate*

1. Demonstrating the Character of God   151
   Salvation does not end with the individual
   The visible quality
   Realism in exhibition
   Personality is central

2. The Legal, but not only the Legal   158
   Human people in our culture
   Personality and culture

Appendices

  A. The Problem of the Middle-Class Church in the Latter Half of the Twentieth Century   163
  B. The Practice of Truth   168

A Word Concerning L'Abri by the Rev. J. A. Kirk   171

Glossary   177

Notes   181

Index   189

SECTION I

The Intellectual and Cultural Climate
of the
Second Half of the Twentieth Century

CHAPTER I

The Gulf is Fixed

BEFORE THE CHASM

The present chasm between the generations has been brought about almost entirely by a change in the concept of truth.

Wherever you look today the new concept holds the field. The consensus about us is almost monolithic, whether you review the arts, literature or just simply read the newspapers and magazines such as *Time, Life, Newsweek, The Listener* or *The Observer*. On every side you can feel the stranglehold of this new methodology—and by 'methodology' we mean the way we approach truth and knowing. It is like suffocating in a particularly bad London fog. And just as fog cannot be kept out by walls or doors, so this consensus comes in around us, till the room we live in is no longer distinct, and yet we hardly realise what has happened.

The tragedy of our situation today is that men and women are being fundamentally affected by the new way of looking at truth and yet they have never even analysed the drift which has taken place. Young people from Christian homes are brought up in the old framework of truth. Then they are subjected to the modern framework. In time they become confused because they do not understand the alternatives with which they are being presented. Confusion becomes bewilderment, and before long they are overwhelmed. This is unhappily true not only of young people, but of many pastors, Christian educators, evangelists and missionaries as well.

So this change in the concept of the way we come to knowledge and truth is the most *crucial problem, as I understand it, facing Christianity today.*

If you had lived in Europe prior to about 1890, or in the United States before about 1935, you would not have had to spend much time, in practice, in thinking about your presuppositions. (These dates may be slightly arbitrary as the change came in Europe, at least, fairly gradually. In America the crucial years of change were from 1913 to 1940 and during these relatively few years the whole way of thinking underwent a revolution—1913 was a most important year in the United States, not because it was the year before the First World War, but for another highly significant reason, as we shall see later.)

Before these dates everyone would have been working on much the same presuppositions, which in practice seemed to accord with the Christian's own presuppositions. This was true both in the area of epistemology and methodology. Now it may be argued that the non-Christian had no right to act on the presuppositions he acted on. That is true. They were being romantic in accepting optimistic answers without a sufficient base. Nevertheless they went on thinking and acting as if these presuppositions were true.

What were these presuppositions? The basic one was that there really are such things as absolutes. They accepted the possibility of an absolute in the area of Being (or knowledge), and in the area of morals. Therefore, because they accepted the possibility of absolutes, though men might disagree as to what these were, nevertheless they could reason together on the classical basis of antithesis. So if anything was true, the opposite was false. In morality, if one thing was right, its opposite was wrong. This little formula, 'If you have A it is not non-A', is the first move in classical logic. If you understand the extent to which this no longer holds sway, you will understand our present situation.

Absolutes imply antithesis. The non-Christian went on romantically operating on this basis without a sufficient base for doing so. Thus it was still possible to discuss what was right and wrong, what was true and false. One could tell a non-Christian to 'be a good girl', and, while she might not have followed your advice, at least she would have understood what you were talking about. To say the same thing to a truly modern girl today would be to make a 'nonsense' statement. The blank look you might receive would not mean that your standards had been rejected but that your message was meaningless.

The shift has been tremendous. Thirty or more years ago you could have said such things as 'This is true' or 'This is right', and you would have been on everybody's wavelength. People may or may not have thought out their beliefs consistently, but everyone would have been talking to each other as though the idea of antithesis was correct. Thus in evangelism, in spiritual matters and in Christian education, you could have begun with the certainty that your audience understood you.

PRESUPPOSITIONAL APOLOGETICS WOULD HAVE STOPPED THE DECAY[1]

It was indeed unfortunate that our Christian 'thinkers', in the time before the shift took place and the chasm was fixed, did not teach and preach with a clear grasp of presuppositions. Had they done this they would not have been taken by surprise, and they could have helped young people to face their difficulties. The really foolish thing is that even now, years after the shift is over, many Christians still do not know what is happening. And this is because they are still not being taught the importance of thinking in terms of presuppositions, especially concerning truth.

The flood-waters of secular thought and the new theology overwhelmed the Church because the leaders did not understand the importance of combating a false set of presuppositions. They largely fought the battle on the wrong ground and so, instead of being far ahead in both defence and communication, they lagged woefully behind. This was a real weakness which it is hard, even today, to rectify among evangelicals.

The use of classical apologetics before this shift took place was effective only because non-Christians were functioning, on the surface, on the same presuppositions, even if they had an inadequate base for them. In classical apologetics though, presuppositions were rarely analysed, discussed or taken into account.

So, if a man got up to preach the Gospel and said, 'Believe this, it is true', those who heard would have said, 'Well, if that is so then its opposite is false'. The presupposition of antithesis invaded men's entire mental outlook. We must not forget that historic Christianity stands on a basis of antithesis. Without it historic Christianity is meaningless.

THE LINE OF DESPAIR

Thus we have a date line like this:

The line of despair——————————————$\begin{cases} \text{Europe about 1890} \\ \text{The U.S. about 1935} \end{cases}$

Notice that I call the line, the line of despair. Above this line we find men living with their romantic notions of absolutes (though with no sufficient logical basis). This side of the line all is changed. Man thinks differently concerning truth, and *so now for us, more than ever before, a presuppositional apologetic is imperative.*

In order to understand this line of despair more clearly, think of it not as a simple horizontal line but as a staircase:

15

The line of despair

PHILOSOPHY
_____
    | ART
    _____
        | MUSIC
        _____
            | GENERAL CULTURE
            _____
                | THEOLOGY

Each of the steps represents a certain stage in time. The higher is earlier, the lower later. It was in this order that the shift in truth affected men's lives.

The shift spread gradually, and in three different ways. People did not suddenly wake up one morning and find that it had permeated everywhere at once.

First of all it spread geographically. The ideas began in Germany and spread outward. They affected the Continent first, then crossed the Channel to England, and then the Atlantic to America. Secondly, it spread through society, from the real intellectual to the more educated, down to the workers, reaching the upper middle class last of all. Thirdly, it spread as represented in the diagram, from one discipline to another, beginning with the philosophers and ending with the theologians. Theology has been last for a long time. It is curious to me, in studying this whole cultural drift, that so many pick up the latest theological fashion and hail it as something new. *But in fact, what the new theology is now saying has already been said previously in each of the other disciplines.*

It is important to grasp the fundamental nature of this line. If we try to evangelise men as though they were above the line when in reality they are this side of it, we will only beat the air. This goes as much for dockers as for intellectuals. The same will be true in the concept of spirituality. This side of the line 'spirituality' becomes exactly opposite to Christian spirituality.

UNITY AND DISUNITY IN RATIONALISM

There is a real unity in non-Christian thought, as well as differences within that unity. The shift below the line of despair is one of the differences within the unity of non-Christian thought. The unifying factor can be called rationalism, or if you prefer, human-ism—though if we use the latter term we must be careful to distinguish its meaning in this context and its meaning in the more limited sense of such a book as *The Humanist Frame*,[2] edited by Sir Julian Huxley. This latter kind of humanism has become a technical term within the larger meaning of the word. Humanism in the inclusive sense is the system whereby man, beginning absolutely by himself, tries rationally to build out from himself, having only man as his integration point, to find all knowledge, meaning and value. Again, the word rationalism, which means the same as humanism in the wider sense, should not be confused with the word rational. Rational means that the things which are about us are not contrary to reason, or, to put it another way, man's aspiration of reason is valid. And so the Judaistic-Christian position is rational, but it is the very antithesis of rationalism.

So rationalism or humanism is the unity within non-Christian thought. Yet if Christians are going to be able to understand and talk to men in their generation they must take account of the form rationalism is currently taking. In one way it is always the same, men trying to build from themselves alone. In another sense it is constantly shifting, with different emphases with which a Christian must be acquainted if he is not to equip himself to work in a period which no longer exists.

The line of despair indicates a titanic shift at this present time within the unity of rationalism. Above the line men were rationalistic optimists. They believed they could begin with themselves and draw a circle which would encompass all thoughts of life, and life itself, without having to depart from the logic of antithesis. They thought that on their own, rationalistically, finite men could find a unity in the total diversity. This is where philosophy stood, prior to our own day. The only real argument between these rationalistic optimists was over the circle that should be drawn. One man would draw a circle and say, 'You can live within this circle'. The next man would cross it out and would draw a different circle. The next man would come along and, crossing out the previous circle, draw his own—*ad infinitum*. So if you start to study philosophy by pursuing the *history* of philosophy, by the time you are through with all these circles, each one of which has been destroyed by the next, you may feel like jumping off London Bridge!

But at a certain point this attempt to spin out a unified optimistic humanism ceased. At this point the philosophers came to the conclusion that they were not going to find a unified rationalistic circle that would contain all thought, and in which they could live. It was as though the rationalist suddenly became trapped in a large round room with no doors and no windows, nothing but complete darkness. From the middle of the room he would feel his way to the walls and begin to look for an exit. Many times he would go round the circumference, and then the terrifying truth would dawn on him that there was no exit, no exit at all! *In the end the philosophers came to the realisation that they could not find this unified rationalistic circle and so, departing from the classical methodology of antithesis, they shifted the concept of truth and modern man was born.*

In this way modern man moved under the line of despair. He was driven to it against his desire. He remained a rationalist, but he had changed. Do we Christians understand this shift in the contemporary world? If we do not understand it then we are largely talking to ourselves.

TENDENCY TOWARDS A UNIFORM CULTURE

The importance of understanding the chasm to which man's thinking has brought him is not of intellectual value alone, but of spiritual value as well. The Christian is to resist the spirit of the world. But when we say this we must understand that the world-spirit does not always take the same form. So the Christian must resist the spirit of the world *in the form it takes in his own generation.* If he does not do this he is not resisting the spirit of the world at all. This is especially so for our generation, as the forces at work against us are of such a total nature. It is our generation of Christians more than any other who need to heed these words which are attributed to Martin Luther:

> If I profess with the loudest voice and clearest exposition every portion of the truth of God except precisely that little point which the world and the devil are at that moment attacking, I am not confessing Christ, however boldly I may be professing Christ. Where the battle rages, there the loyalty of the soldier is proved, and to be steady on all the battlefield besides, is mere flight and disgrace if he flinches at that point.

It would be false to say that there is always a totally uniform culture. This is not so. And yet, as we study the art and literature of the past, and those things which help us to understand a culture, we find that there tends to be a drift towards a monolithic and uniform whole.

Through a study of archaeology it is possible to show how a certain idea developed in one place and then over a period of several hundred years spread over wide areas. One could give as an example the Indo-European culture, whose spread can be traced through the flow of certain words.

In the distant past it took so long for cultural concepts to spread that by the time they had reached other areas they had sometimes already changed in their place of origin. But today the world is small and it is very possible to have a monolithic culture spreading rapidly and influencing great sections of mankind. No artificial barriers, such as the Iron Curtain, can keep out the flow of these ideas. As the world has shrunk, and as it has become post-Christian, both sides of the Iron Curtain have followed the same methodology and the same basic monolithic thought-form, namely the lack of absolutes and antithesis leading to pragmatic relativism.

In our modern forms of specialised education there is a tendency to lose the whole in the parts, and in this sense we can say that our generation produces few truly educated men. True education means thinking by association across the various disciplines, and not just being highly qualified in one field, as a technician might be. I suppose no discipline has tended to think more in fragmented fashion than the orthodox or evangelical theology of today.

Those standing in the stream of historic Christianity have been especially slow to understand the relationships between various areas of thought. When the Apostle warned us to 'keep ourselves — unspotted from the world',[3] he was not talking of some abstraction. If the Christian is to apply this injunction to himself he must understand what confronts him antagonistically in his own moment of history. Otherwise he simply becomes a useless museum piece and not a living warrior for Jesus Christ.

The orthodox Christian has paid a very heavy price, both in the defence and communication of the Gospel, for his failure to think and act as an educated man at grips with the uniformity of our modern culture.

CHAPTER 2

The First Step in the Line of Despair: Philosophy

HEGEL, THE DOORWAY

It was the German philosopher Hegel (1770–1831) who became the first man to open the door into the line of despair. Before his time truth was conceived on the basis of antithesis, not for any adequate reason but because man romantically acted upon it.

Truth, in the sense of antithesis, is related to the idea of cause and effect. Cause and effect produces a chain reaction which goes straight on in a horizontal line. With the coming of Hegel all this changed.

We must understand the importance of timing. What Hegel taught arrived at just the right moment of history for his thinking to have its maximum effect.[1]

Imagine that Hegel was sitting one day in the local tavern, surrounded by his friends, conversing on the philosophical issues of the day. Suddenly he put down his mug of beer on the table and said, 'I have a new idea. From now on let us think in this way; instead of thinking in terms of cause and effect, what we really have is a thesis, and opposite is an antithesis, and the answer to their relationship is not in the horizontal movement of cause and effect, but the answer is always synthesis.' Now suppose also that a hard-headed German business man had been standing by and had overheard his remark. He might have thought, 'How abstruse and impractical!' But he could not have been further from the truth. Because whether Hegel himself or those listening understood it to be the case, when Hegel propounded this idea he changed the world.

It has never been the same since. If one understands the development of philosophy, or morals, or political thought from that day to this, one knows that Hegel and synthesis have won. In other words, Hegel has removed the straight line of previous thought and in its place he has substituted a triangle. Instead of antithesis we have, as modern man's approach to truth, synthesis.

We say that Hegel was only the door into the line of despair. He himself never went below it. A good case can be made for thinking that he remained an idealist. He thought that in practice synthesis could be arrived at by reason. But this did not prove possible and so the next man we have to consider went below the line.

KIERKEGAARD, THE FIRST MAN BELOW

It is often said that Søren Kierkegaard, the Dane (1813–55), is the father of all modern thinking. And so he is. He is the father of modern secular thinking and of the new theological thinking. Our diagram now looks like this:

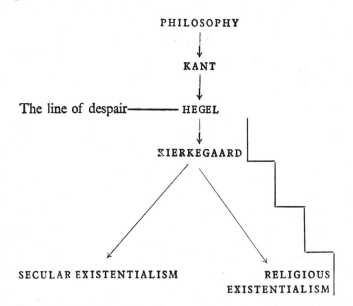

Why is it that Kierkegaard can so aptly be thought of as the father of both? What proposition did he add to Hegel's thought that made the difference? Kierkegaard came to the conclusion that you could not arrive at synthesis by reason. Instead, you achieved everything of real importance by a leap of faith. So he separated absolutely the rational and logical from faith. The reasonable and faith bear no relationship to each other, like this:

FAITH
———————————————————————
THE RATIONAL AND THE LOGICAL

It is not our purpose here to discuss all that Kierkegaard taught. There was much more than this. We might, for example, debate

21

with profit whether or not he was a real Christian. Or whether, if he came back today, he would be pleased with what had been made of his teaching. *But the important thing about him is that, when he put forth the concept of a leap of faith, he became in a real way the father of all modern existential thought, both secular and theological.*

As a result of this, from that time on, if rationalistic man wants to deal with the real things of human life (such as purpose, significance, the validity of love) he must discard rational thought about them and make a gigantic, non-rational leap of faith. The rationalistic framework had failed to produce an answer on the basis of reason, and so all hope of a uniform field of knowledge had to be abandoned. We get the resulting dichotomy like this:

THE NON-RATIONAL AND NON-LOGICAL	Existential experience; the final experience; the first-order experience.
THE RATIONAL AND LOGICAL	Only particulars, no purpose, no meaning. Man is a machine.

Once we appreciate the development of modern philosophy in this way, we may note that, though there appear to be many forms of philosophy today, in reality there are very few. They have a uniform cast about them. You might listen, on the one hand, to the defining philosophy as taught in Cambridge, and then turn, on the other hand, to the existentialism of, say, Karl Jaspers, and think there was no unity between them. But this is not so. There is one basic agreement in almost all of the Chairs of Philosophy today, and that is a radical denial of the possibility of putting forth a circle which will encompass all. In this sense the philosophies of today can be called in all seriousness anti-philosophies.

THE EXISTENTIALISM OF JASPERS, SARTRE AND HEIDEGGER

In the two halves of existential thinking which we said flowed from Kierkegaard we will pick up first that of the secular. Later we will pick up the theological in considering Karl Barth.

There are three main schools of secular existentialist thinking: The Swiss, the French and the German. Most people do not know the work of Karl Jaspers (b. 1883) in Switzerland as well as that of the French or German, but he is an exceedingly important man. He is German, but now teaches at the University of Basle. He lays a great deal of emphasis on the need to wait for a non-rational 'final experience', which would give meaning to life. People who follow Jaspers have come to me and said, 'I have had a final experience'. They never expect me to ask them what it was. The simple fact is that, if I asked such a thing, it would prove that I was among the uninitiated.

The fact that it is an *existential* experience means that it cannot be communicated. It is not possible to communicate content with regard to the experience which they have had. Some of these men have sat down with me and said, 'It is obvious from looking at you and talking to you, from noticing your sensitivity and sympathy with others, and the openness of your approach to men, that you too are a man who knows the reality of final experience.' They mean this as a supreme compliment, and I always say, 'Thank you very much indeed'. And I mean it, because it is quite remarkable to have one of these men say to an orthodox Christian that they think he understands. But then I go on to say to them, 'Yes, I have had a final experience, but it can be verbalised, and it is of a nature that can be rationally discussed.' Then I talk of my personal relationship with the personal God who is there. I try to make them understand that this relationship is based on God's written, propositional communication to men, and on the finished work of Jesus Christ in space-time history. They reply that this is impossible, that I am trying to do something that cannot be done. The discussion goes on from there.

Try to put yourself for a moment in such a man's place. He has a deep problem, for he hangs everything to do with his certainty of being and the hope of significance upon some titanic experience he had at a specific point in the past.

It would be wrong to imagine that these men are not serious. I wish many evangelicals had the integrity these men show in their struggles. I have been told that when Karl Jaspers begins his lectures to his best students he warns them that they must not commit suicide, because it cannot be certain that one has a final experience by taking one's own life. Perhaps we might wish that many Christians who say they believe in Christ had such intensity of commitment.

But in their struggles there is a horror of great darkness. Though they may be people of great sincerity, this does not of itself make them able to communicate to others their experience. Nor can the individual verbalise to himself what has happened. Tomorrow morning they may say, 'Yesterday I had an experience'. The day after they still say, 'I had an experience'. A month and a year later they are hanging on grimly to their only hope of significance and certainty of being by repeating, 'I know I had an experience'. The horror of this situation is due to their putting their hope on a non-rational, non-logical, non-communicable experience.

23

If we move from Switzerland to France we come to Jean-Paul Sartre (b. 1905) and Albert Camus (1913–60). They differ and yet share the same basic concepts. Sartre, perhaps, speaks the more clearly of the two. He says that we live in an absurd universe. The total, he says, is ridiculous. Nevertheless you try to authenticate yourself by an act of the will. It does not really matter in which direction you act as long as you act.

Let us take the field of morals as a good example of the direction of his thought. You see an old lady and if you help her safely across the road you have 'authenticated yourself'. But if you choose to beat her over the head and snatch her handbag, you would equally have 'authenticated yourself'. The content is unimportant, you just *choose* and *act*. That is it, you have authenticated yourself. This is existentialism in its French form. As I shall show later, neither Sartre nor Camus have been able to live this out in practice, but it is their theoretical position.

How is it that these men get to such a strange position? It is because they have gone below the line of despair. They have given up the hope of a rational circle to give an answer to life, and are left with only the anti-rational. It makes not the slightest difference to the final outcome if you dress up your problem with theological words—the problem remains equally acute.

Finally we have the German form of existentialism, as it is propounded by Martin Heidegger (b. 1889). The fascinating thing about Heidegger is that there are two distinct periods in his life. The first period takes him up to the age of about seventy, and the second from then on till the present. Some of my students have joked about this, and made up a song abot how, 'The old Heidegger is the new Heidegger!' The change came because he could no longer live on the basis of his system. Before the change, which we will consider more closely later, Heidegger was a true existentialist. He came to the same need for authentication as Sartre. How was this to be achieved? Not by an act of the *will*, but by a vague *feeling* of dread. Dread is not to be confused with fear. To him fear has an object; dread has not. Authentication comes through feeling the dread, *Angst*, of something that is beyond your comprehension—a foreboding, and that is all.

THE ANTI-PHILOSOPHY OF THE ANGLO-SAXON WORLD

Two main types of philosophy have recently held the field in the Anglo-Saxon world. They are logical positivism and defining philosophy. Neither of these are rooted in existentialism, indeed both would claim to differ sharply from existentialism. They would strongly insist that they were logical and rational. While we would concede that they are not related in origin to existentialism, nevertheless they have this in common: in their different ways they are all anti-philosophies.

Logical positivism claims to lay the foundation for each step as it goes along, in a rational way. Yet in reality it puts forth no theoretical universal to validate its very first step. Positivists accept that, though they present no logical reason why this should be so, what reaches them from the 'outside' may be called 'data', i.e. has objective validity.

This dilemma was well illustrated by a young man who had been studying logical positivism at Oxford. He was with us in Switzerland as a student in Farel House, and he said one day, 'I'm confused about some of these things. I would like to lead a seminar and see how this whole matter stands.' So he did. When he began he said, 'Well, when this data reaches you . . .'

At once I said, 'How do you know, on the basis of logical positivism, that it is data?'

He started again, and went on for another sentence or two, and then said a second time, 'When this data reaches you . . .'

I felt very much that I was slapping a child's hands when it reaches over into the box of chocolates; but I had to say, 'No, you must not use the word data, it is loaded with all kinds of meaning, it assumes there is objectivity and your system has never proved it.'

'What do I say then?' he replied.

So I said, 'Just say blip. You don't know what you mean by data, so substitute blip.'

He began once more, 'When blip reaches you . . .' and the discussion was over. On the basis of their form of rationalism there is just as much logic in calling the something 'blip' as 'data'.

Thus, in its own way, though it uses the title of positivism, it is just as much a leap of faith, having no postulated circle within which to act, as existentialism.

However, the defining philosophy is more important in England and the United States today and is gaining in strength.

The starting-point with those who subscribe to this philosophy is, as the title suggests, definition. They say they will on no account take any first step without rationally and logically defining the terms they use. And they will go no further than can be accurately defined.

This is all very well, but even if we overlook the differences in their own ranks as to whether their categories are accurate or not, they still have other problems. Many of them would agree that all their work is no more than prologomena. They start off by defining terms in the hope that one day some of the random pieces may be fitted together. Now this is good, in so far as they have demonstrated that some problems cease to exist when they have carefully defined the terms involved. In providing a tool for careful thinking their work has also been most helpful. But they are carefully defining terms, without dealing with meaning and purpose. Classical philosophy through Kant consisted of two parts. It dealt, certainly, with details. But the details were to be set within a circle which it was claimed could contain all knowledge and life. But this defining philosophy deals with the details only. It would not claim to be a system. In this sense, as a contrast to classical philosophy, it is an anti-philosophy.

Then secondly, many of these men also have their own personal leap of faith. As defining philosophers they have a prestige in their own field. On the other hand, many of these men take a strong position for optimistic humanism.[2] That is, many of them would make the same optimistic statements as a man like Sir Julian Huxley. But what they are doing is this: they are using their prestige as careful instructors in the art of defining philosophy in order to enhance the strength of their humanistic view regarding man. But it should be observed that weight of scholarship in defining words does not make up for weakness of argument in the larger questions. In fact there is no bridge at all between their limited philosophy, which says nothing about meaning or purpose, and their optimistic statements. They have leapt over the gap between the two by faith. However careful and rational their definitions of words may be, their observation on man, in that it is optimistic humanism, is unadulterated faith.

And the evolutionary humanism as a whole, which is current today, is in the same plight. Anyone can assert with all the persuasion at his command that man is due for a rosy future. But this again is a leap of faith, if there is no point of observation, either clinically or sociologically, to demonstrate that man will be better tomorrow than he was yesterday or is today.

Sir Julian Huxley has taken such a purely optimistic answer one step further by stating that man will only be improved by accepting a new mystique. Thus he suggests that society will function better if it has a religion, even though no god really exists.[3] For example, he says:

From the specifically religious point of view, the desirable direction of evolution might be defined as the divinisation of existence—but for this to have operative significance we must

26

frame a new definition of 'the divine' free from all connotations of external supernatural beings.

Religion today is imprisoned in a theistic frame of ideas, compelled to operate in the unrealities of the dualistic world. In the unitary humanist frame it acquires a new look and new freedom. With the aid of our new vision it has the opportunity of escaping from the theistic impasse and of playing its proper role in the real world of unitary existence.

Now it may be true that it can be shown by observation that society copes better with life through believing that there is a god. But, in that case, surely optimistic humanism is being essentially unreasonable (and, like the others we have discussed, shows exactly the same irrational leap of faith) if, in order to be optimistic, it rests upon the necessity of mankind believing and functioning upon a lie.

THE USE OF DRUGS

It is not only the existentialist who has talked about an experience as a means of validating oneself. Right up to the time of his death Aldous Huxley suggested that a way of achieving what he described as a 'first order experience' would be through drugs.[4] This experience would, like the final experience advocated by the existentialists, be above the line of rational validation, in this way:

THE NON-RATIONAL AND NON-LOGICAL	A first-order experience by the use of drugs.
THE RATIONAL AND LOGICAL	No purpose or meaning found.

This overwhelming desire for some non-rational experience is responsible for most of the serious use of the drugs L.S.D. and S.T.P. at this time. With the sensitive person drugs are today not usually used for escape. On the contrary he hopes that, by taking them, he will experience the reality of something which will give his life some meaning. Professor Timothy Leary, formerly of Harvard University, has intriguingly linked up the L.S.D. experience with that described in the *Tibetan Book of the Dead*.[5] Thus he shows that the desire for, and the form of, this experience changes very little from West to East. Whether it is the existentialist speaking, or Aldous Huxley, or Eastern mysticism, we find a uniform need for an irrational experience to make some sense

27

of life. Their views have brought them to a wall and by an unrelated leap of faith they hope to clear the wall. Each of their views may be separated in detailed description but they have come to the same wall and are making the same attempt to clear it. Each case involves a non-rational leap of faith.

The Chairs of Philosophy in most universities have come under the line of despair. The living philosophical discussions have tended to move into unusual settings—such as philosophic astronomy, modern jazz, or among the real hippies. It is in such fields as these that philosophy is being beaten out. Academic philosophy as such, including Anglo-Saxon philosophy, is today almost entirely anti-philosophy.

In concluding this section let us note that when we speak of being under the line of despair, we do not mean that these men necessarily sit down and weep, but that they have given up all hope of achieving a rational unified answer to knowledge and life.

WHAT DOES AND DOES NOT HAPPEN IN THESE EXPERIENCES

It is obvious that often when a man claims to have had an experience, whether under drugs or not, something has certainly happened to him. When he experiences, for example, the 'redness' of a red rose, he has really touched something. But what?

Usually only two live options are presented as to what happens in an Eastern religious experience, an existential experience, or a drug experience. One is told either that they have stumbled on 'nothing' in their experience, or else that they have met 'the reality of god'. This latter is especially true when the Eastern religious experience is under consideration. The *guru* says, 'I have met something'. Usually people describe it as nonsense or say that he has 'met god'.

The built-in trouble with all these existential experiences is that the content of such an experience is not open to communication. Only the unknowing would demand, 'Please describe to me in normal categories what you have experienced.'

But I believe that there is a third live option when we ask ourselves what these people have touched. It is an alternative explanation Christians can give because we see these people *as they really are* in God's universe.

God has created a real, external world. It is not an extension of His essence. That real, external world exists. God has also created man as a real, personal being and he possesses a 'mannishness' from which he can never escape. On the basis of their own world-view often these experience-seekers are neither sure the external

28

world is there, nor that man as man is there. But I have come to the conclusion that, despite their intellectual doubts, many of them *have had* a true experience of the reality of the external world that exists, and/or the 'mannishness' that exists. They can do this precisely because this is how God has made man, in His own image, able to experience the real world and man's 'mannishness'. Thus they have hit upon something which exists, and it is neither nothing, nor is it God. We might sum up this third alternative by saying that when they experience the 'redness' of the rose, they are having the same kind of experience of the external world as the farmer who ploughs his field. They are both touching the world that is.

In the same way, lovers on the left bank of the Seine in Paris experience the 'mannishness' of man when they fall in love and yet cry because they do not believe love exists. If I met any of these I would put my hand gently on their shoulders and say, 'You will be lost forever, bound for Hell, if you do not accept Christ as your Saviour, but at this moment you understand something real about the universe. Though your system may say love does not exist, your own experience shows that it does.' They have not touched the personal God who exists, but, for a fleeting moment, they have touched the existence of true personality in their love. This is indeed an objective reality, because God has made their personalities in this way. It is true that in these experiences man has touched something, not nothing, but what he has touched is not God but the objective reality of the external world and the 'mannishness' of man that God has created.

Some have wondered why Christians should not use drugs since drugs do sharpen perception. But the price paid for increased perception is much too great. A short while ago an anonymous poem was published in *The Listener* based on the 23rd Psalm. It began:

> King Heroin is my shepherd, I shall always want,
> He maketh me to lie down in the gutters.
> He leadeth me beside the troubled waters.
> He destroyeth my soul.

With the exception of their use for medical purposes, and therefore under careful control, drugs are destructive. Playing with drugs is foolish, as well as wrong.

CHAPTER 3

The Second Step—Art

If it is true that philosophy, the first step in the line of despair, touched only a few people, art, the second step, influenced very many more.

As in philosophy so in art there is a doorway into the line, and this is provided by the Impressionists. When they began they did not see themselves as rebelling against classic concepts. They were interested in a study of light, as was the Englishman Turner who had preceded them. But later their work, especially the work of Monet, changed and expressed the new mentality.

VAN GOGH AND GAUGUIN

There are three men who stand out above all. They are Van Gogh the Dutchman, Gauguin and Cézanne the Frenchmen. They are the three pillars of modern art. In each case they tried to find a universal in their art as Leonardo Da Vinci[1] had tried many centuries before them. What the philosopher was trying to do within the scope of the whole universe they now tried to do on a limited scale on their canvases. As they came to understand that they had gone over the threshold of the line of despair these men began a desperate search to find a universal that would give them back reality, something more than just particulars. They were seeking to express a form and a freedom which would be valid in the scope of their discipline, art.

Van Gogh (1853–90) can be thought of first. Very often people say he committed suicide because he was mentally ill or because Gauguin stole a woman he was interested in. These may have been contributing factors, but the suicide was due to a much more basic problem. There may have been psychological problems, but the final explosion came as a result of disillusionment on a much more fundamental issue. Van Gogh thought to make a new religion in which the sensitive people, the artists, would blaze the trail. For this purpose he dreamt of starting an artistic community in Arles where he was living. He was joined by Gauguin, but after a few months they began to quarrel violently. Van Gogh's hope of his new religion was gone and soon after, he committed suicide. The death of hope in man had taken place in Van Gogh. He died in despair.

Gauguin (1848–1903) did the same thing. He too was seeking for a universal. He went to Tahiti and there he championed the idea of the noble savage. The savage was to be the return to the primitive, the child of the race, and it was here, going back in time, that he hoped to find the universal. So Gauguin began to paint the beauty of the women he found there. For a time he felt that he had successfully removed himself from the loss of innocence in civilisation, and that this was enough. But his last great painting tells the conclusion he came to eventually.

This painting is called, *What? Whence? Whither?*[2] and it hangs now in the Boston Museum of Art. The title is painted on a yellow corner on the upper left of the picture, thus making quite sure that anyone who looks at the work will understand its meaning. Elsewhere[3] in discussing the painting he tells us that we are to look at it the opposite way to normal, namely from the right to the left. So at the right, where we look first, we see the same kind of beauty as in his other paintings. There is the same exotic symbolism, the same appeal to the sensuous in the concept of the noble savage. But by the time our eye has moved across the canvas to the far left we see a very different end to the story. He began the painting in 1897 and finished it in 1898. This is what he says about it: 'I have finished a philosophical work on this theme, comparable to the Gospel . . . A figure lifts up its arms into the air and, astonished, looks at these two personages who dare to think of their destination.' A little farther on he continues:

'Whither? Close to the death of an old woman, a strange, stupid bird concludes: What? . . . The eternal problem that punishes our pride. O Sorrow, thou art my master. Fate how cruel thou art, and always vanquished, I revolt.'[4] When you look at the left-hand side of the picture you see three figures. The first is a young Tahitian woman in all her beauty. Beside her is a poor old woman dying, watched only by a monstrous bird, which has no counterpart in nature. When Gauguin finished this painting he too tried to commit suicide, though in fact he did not succeed.

Both of these two men were attempting to find a humanistic universal. They failed dismally and are left below the line of despair.

It was in the basic geometrical form that Cézanne (1839–1906) attempted to discover his universal. Many of his landscape paintings look like a taut diaphragm, a diaphragm pulled over geometric forms. As far as we know tragedy never caught up with him. He died, as far as I have been able to discover, without ever coming to the conclusion of despair.

But someone else carried on from where he left off. Picasso (born 1881) saw the work of Cézanne at the large exhibitions of his work in Paris in 1905 and 1907, and discussed the problems involved in Gertrude Stein's home in that same city, where many painters used to gather.

Picasso brought together the noble savage of Gauguin, the geometric form of Cézanne, and also incorporated something from the African masks that had just become known in Paris, developing between 1906 and 1911 what was to be called Cubism. The great picture of 1906–07 *Les Demoiselles d'Avignon* (now in the Museum of Modern Art, New York) shows this development. The women on the left are much like those he painted before, but already showing Cézanne's influence in an exaggerated form; but when one turns to the women on the right, one finds that instead of their being women, they have become demonic beings and symbols as in the African masks. Their humanity has been lost.

Picasso then pushed further. Unlike, say, Renoir, who painted his wife in such a way that she could be recognised (that is, the subject was a particular), Picasso was seeking for a universal. As he abstracted further one cannot tell whether his women are blondes or brunettes. This is a move towards the universal and away from the particular. But if you go far enough your abstracted women can become 'all women' or even everything. But the difficulty is that when you get to that point the viewer has no clue what he is looking at. You have succeeded in making your own world on your canvas, and in this sense you have become god. But at the same time you have lost contact with the person who views your painting. We have come to the position where we cannot communicate. The problem of modern man's loss of communication and his alienation did not have to wait for the computers and cybernetics. Picasso, the modern man, exhibited this at this time in his art.

Picasso 'solved' his problem with a romantic leap. One day he fell in love and because he felt the force of love he wrote on the canvases, 'J'aime Eva' (I love Eva).[5] The painting could have been of anything, a chair or something else abstracted. But suddenly, with the words sprawled across the picture, he was in touch again with the man who looked on. But the communication has absolutely no logical relationship to the subject of his canvas. Picasso has failed: his abstraction carried to its logical conclusion has left him with no communication. What remains to him is that which, in his world-view, is a leap.

This is modern man. This is the concept of truth by which we are surrounded. This is the spirit of the world to which we must say 'No', no matter what face it puts on, including a theological one. This is that which makes the chasm between the last generation and our generation a break of more than 400 years; a greater break than that between the Renaissance and the generation before ours. The tragedy is not only that these talented men have reached the point of despair, but that so many who look on and admire really do not understand. They are influenced by the concepts, and yet they have never analysed what it all means.

MONDRIAN

Mondrian (1872–1944) picked up Picasso's position in art and developed Picasso's style to an extreme conclusion. Mondrian's horizontals and verticals are lovely and magnificent. In architecture they have been used as a practical form. However, for him they were not just horizontals and verticals for he too was fighting for a universal.

One day I went to the museum in Zürich. They have a big collection of modern paintings there. I went into one of the rooms and I was aghast. There was a Mondrian with a frame on it. Mondrian did not put frames on his pictures. So I went to the office and asked the man in charge if the Mondrian had a frame on it when he received it. He replied, 'No, we put it on.' So I said, 'Don't you understand? If Mondrian came in here he would just smash the picture against the wall.' As far as I could tell this was a new idea to him. Really this man did not seem to understand the picture in his museum, because Mondrian's whole concept was the building of a universal.

Mondrian painted his pictures and hung them on the wall. They were frameless so that they would not look like holes in the wall. As the pictures conflicted with the room, he had to make a new room. So Mondrian had furniture made for him, particularly by Rietveld, a member of De Stijl, and Van der Leck. There was an exhibition in the Stedelijk Museum in Amsterdam in July–September, 1951, called 'De Stijl', where this could be seen. As you looked you were led to admire the balance between room and furniture, in just the same way as there is such a good balance in his individual pictures. But if a man came into that room there would be no place for him. It is a room for abstract balance, but not for man. This is the conclusion modern man has reached, below the line of despair. He has tried to build a system out from himself, but this system has come to the place where there is no room in the universe for man.

DADA, MARCEL DUCHAMP, THE HAPPENINGS AND THE ENVIRONMENTS

I have a poem that appeared on page one of the last issue of the magazine called *De Stijl*[6] which was published by the De Stijl school of painting with which Mondrian was connected. It is written by Hans Arp (b. 1887), one of the members of the original Dada group. This is a translation from the German:

> the head downward
> the legs upward
> he tumbles into the bottomless
> from whence he came
>
> he has no more honour in his body
> he bites no more bite of any short meal
> he answers no greeting
> and is not proud when being adored
>
> the head downward
> the legs upward
> he tumbles into the bottomless
> from whence he came
>
> like a dish covered with hair
> like a four-legged sucking chair
> like a deaf echotrunk
> half full half empty
>
> the head downward
> the legs upward
> he tumbles into the bottomless
> from whence he came.

On the basis of modern man's methodology, whether expressed in philosophy, art, literature or theology, there can be no other ending than this—man tumbling into the bottomless.

Dada is a chance concept. The very word was chosen by chance. One day some people flipped through a French dictionary in Zürich. They put a finger down at random and found it rested on the word dada. It means a rocking-horse. And so it was by blind chance that they conceived the name for their school of art.

In the same way they composed their poems. They cut printed words out of the newspaper, threw them in a hat and picked them out by chance. But these men were deadly serious; it really was no game they were playing.

One of these men was Marcel Duchamp (b. 1887), whom every Christian ought to know about. He could be called the high-priest of destruction. He is best known for his picture *Nude descending a stairway*, which is now in the Philadelphia Museum of Art. He is brilliant and destructive—and he means to destroy. He will seek to destroy you from within yourself. The best collection of his work in the world is at the Philadelphia Museum of Art. There is a picture in the Museum of Modern Art in New York, *Le passage de la vierge à la mariée* (the words are written on the canvas and mean 'The passage of the virgin to the married state'). Naturally every man or woman who goes to look at the picture tries to find in the picture something which relates to its title. But no matter how long one looks one finds no picture of a virgin, nor of a virgin becoming a married woman. Thus he causes the viewer to make himself dirty.

He is the man who, about 1960, gave birth to the *happenings*, and then beyond this the *environments*. The happenings began in New York. We might say that, though America was behind at the time of the Armory Show in 1913, today, in modern art and in many other areas under the line of despair, she leads the world.

In the happenings you are put as it were within the picture. You look at people acting; and, as the observer, you are forced to participate. There is always a nonsense element, and there is usually a dirty action as well. Always the observer is involved and is deliberately destroyed.

What are they saying? Everything is chance. Chance, the nothingness is not just shut up in a framed picture but it is the entire structure of life. You are in the chance, in the nothingness. You are the destroyed ones.

A good example of the Environment was some of the rooms in the art show, 'Art Zero, Art Nul,' held in the Stedelijk Museum, Amsterdam, in the summer of 1965. It was the most important show held on the Continent at the time. One entered the rooms in the gallery and looked at objects. But there was something more than mere looking at individual objects, rather you felt permeated by a total context which was almost subliminal. Almost against your wish you got drawn into the mood of the room. I watched young couples going through these rooms in Amsterdam. I knew that most of them did not understand what they saw. But I was certain that by the time they came out, the atmosphere would have had its effect and their moral defences would have been weakened. They were touched at a deeper level than only the mind, and, though the girl could not perhaps analyse what she saw, yet surely she would be more ready to say 'Yes' by the time she came out.

In this connection it is important to note that the leaders of the Provos, and anarchist movement in Amsterdam which has been much in the international news through 1966 and 1967, say that this movement is the logical result of the exposition programme at the Stedelijk Museum in Amsterdam through the last fifteen years. It is also interesting to note that the Provos call their public demonstrations 'Happenings'.

These paintings, these poems and these demonstrations which we have been talking about are the expression of men who are struggling with their appalling lostness. Dare we laugh at such things? Dare we feel superior when we view their tortured expressions in their art? Christians should stop laughing and take such men seriously. Then we shall have the right to speak again to our generation. These men are dying while they live, yet where is our compassion for them? There is nothing more ugly than an orthodoxy without understanding or without compassion.

CHAPTER 4

The Third and Fourth Steps—Music and the General Culture

Just as in philosophy and art, there is a doorway into the line of despair in music as well. Debussy (1862–1918) is the doorway into the field of modern music. It is not as easy to trace the steps in music as it is in visual art, yet the parallels are there. It is not as easy because, inevitably, music has a more subjective element in it. Nevertheless the general trend from Debussy until now is clear enough.

An exhaustive study, which we cannot undertake here, would involve considering jazz as well as classical music. Such a consideration would involve discussing the shift in form and content in the 20's and 30's when jazz was introduced into the white man's culture, and how the jazz of the 40's was the doorway to the despair of much modern jazz.[1]

But we will turn our attention to music more in line with the classical tradition. A few illustrations must suffice for the whole. There could be much discussion of detail in this and yet the total direction of movement is clear. In a later chapter I will deal with the music of John Cage. Here I want to look at musique concrète.

MUSIQUE CONCRÈTE

This was developed by Pierre Schaeffer (b. 1910) in Paris. Musique concrète is not electronic music, that is music made electronically and therefore consisting of sounds one does not normally hear. Musique concrète is real sound, but seriously distorted. In the beginning it was created by jumping grooves on a phonographic record. Later Pierre Schaeffer invented a machine by which the distortions can be carefully controlled. With his machine he can lift out the source of the sound, split it up, reverse it, slow it down or speed it up, in fact do just about anything to alter it. To hear the result is to begin to distrust your ears, just as in Op Art you begin to distrust your eyes. The effect is over-whelming. The message which comes across from the distortion is the same as in modern painting. All is relative, nothing is sure, nothing is fixed, all is in flux. Musique concrète is just one more way of presenting the uniform message of modern man.

UNESCO has put out a record, entitled *Premier panorama de Musique Concrète*.[2] In it is a clear example of what these men are doing, including a selection by one of Schaeffer's friends, Pierre Henry.

He uses the human voice speaking Greek. Greek, of course, is exactly the right language to speak in such a setting, for it is the language representative of our Western culture. The voice is first built up out of chance sounds, reflecting modern man's view that man who verbalises arose by chance in a chance universe with only a future of chance ahead of him. Henry portrays this remorse-lessly in sound. Suddenly something else begins to happen; the voice begins to degenerate and to fall apart. It is as though one is watching a beautiful woman die and totally decompose before one's eyes. But in this case it is not just the physical body but the whole man who rots away. It begins to shiver, to shake, to be corrupted. It begins with chance sounds, goes on to the Greek and ends in chaos. *There can be no other terminus when antithesis dies, when relativism is born and when the possibility of finding any universal which would make sense of the particulars is denied.* This is the consensus of the cultural environment, and this is that world-spirit which we must reject and into which we must speak.

HENRY MILLER

With this American novelist (b. 1891) we begin our consideration of the fourth step in the line of despair, which I have named general culture. This could be divided into a number of steps but I have placed these subjects together under this heading for convenience.

Young people often say that the writing of Henry Miller is not just pornographic but is a philosophical statement. Parents of these young people ask me whether I agree. I reply, 'Yes, your child is right. They are certainly dirty books and because of this will soil you. However, they are not intended to be mere porno-graphy. Miller is an anti-law writer. He smashes everything to pieces so that there is nothing left. Even sex is smashed. This is especially devastating because it is often in the sexual area of life that men hope to find some kind of meaning when they have abandoned the search elsewhere.'

Not only with Miller but also with other modern writers we can appreciate the result of this as we notice how they use the girl in their books. The playmate becomes the plaything, and we are right back with the Marquis de Sade. (I want to talk about the new changed Henry Miller a little farther on.)

PHILOSOPHIC HOMOSEXUALITY

Some forms of homosexuality today are of a similar nature, in that they are not just homosexuality but a philosophic expression. One must have understanding for the real homophile's problem. But much modern homosexuality is an expression of the current denial of antithesis. It has led in this case to an obliteration of the distinction between man and woman. So the male and the female as complementary partners are finished. This is a form of homosexuality which is a part of the movement below the line of despair. But this is not an isolated problem; it is a part of the world-spirit of the generation which surrounds us. It is imperative that Christians realise the conclusions which are being drawn as a result of the death of absolutes.

JOHN OSBORNE

In the area of drama, another aspect of general culture, it is important to consider John Osborne (b. 1929), one of the Angry Young Men. In many ways he is a great playwright, but he has been accurately described as an idealist who has not been able to find an ideal. This is a magnificent description. Osborne is a man of temperament, courage and sensitivity; a man to ride on a charger with his lance at the ready into the great battles of life. He is an idealist by choice, but without an ideal: a man who cares and yet has found nothing worth caring about. His whole approach is summed up with magnificent clarity in his play *Martin Luther*. As history it has weaknesses, but in general it portrays the early part of Luther's life with considerable accuracy. But the moment of truth comes with great force at the very end. Luther is standing with one of his babies in his arms. The elderly head of Luther's old monastery comes to visit him. They face each other. The old man says, 'Martin, do you know you are right?' And against all history Osborne makes him reply, 'Let's hope so.' The lights come on, the curtain is down and the play is finished. The drama critic of *The Times* understood. He said, 'Isn't it interesting that he had to put in that last line to make it a twentieth century play!'

When we review modern poetry as part of our own general culture we find the same tendency to despair. Near the time of his death, Dylan Thomas (1914–53) wrote a poem called, *Elegy*.[3] He did not actually put it together himself so we cannot be too sure of the exact order of the stanzas. But the way it is given below is probably the right order. This poem is by a fellow human being of our generation. He is not an insect on the head of a pin, but shares the same flesh and blood as we do, a man of today in real despair:

Too proud to die, broken and blind he died
The darkest way, and did not turn away,
A cold kind man brave in his narrow pride

On that darkest day, Oh, forever may
He lie lightly, at last, on the last, crossed
Hill, under the grass, in love, and there grow

Young among the long flocks, and never lie lost
Or still all the numberless days of his death, though
Above all he longed for his mother's breast.

Which was rest and dust, and in the kind ground
The darkest justice of death, blind and unblessed.
Let him find no rest but be fathered and found.

I prayed in the crouching room, by his blind bed,
In the muted house, one minute before
Noon, and night, and light. The rivers of the dead

Veined his poor hand I held, and I saw
Through his unseeing eyes to the roots of the sea.
(An old tormented man three-quarters blind),

I am not too proud to cry that He and he
will never never go out of my mind.
All his bones crying, and poor in all but pain,

Being innocent, he dreaded that he died
Hating his God, but what he was was plain:
An old kind man brave in his burning pride.

The sticks of the house were his; his books he owned.
Even as a baby he had never cried;
Nor did he now, save to his secret wound.

Out of his eyes I saw the last light glide.
Here among the light of the lording sky
An old blind man is with me where I go

Walking in the meadow of his son's eye
On whom a world of ills came down like snow.
He cried as he died, fearing at last the spheres'

Last sound, the world going out without a breath:
Too proud to cry, too frail to check the tears,
And caught between two nights, blindness and death.

O deepest wound of all that he should die
On that darkest day. Oh, he could hide
The tears out of his eyes, too proud to cry.

Until I die he will not leave my side.

In the Festival Hall in London, in one of the higher galleries in the rear corridor, there is a bronze of Dylan Thomas. Anyone who can look at it without compassion is dead. There he faces you with a cigarette at the side of his mouth, the very cigarette hung in despair. It is not good enough to take a man like this or any of the others and smash them as though we have no responsibility for them. This is sensitivity crying out in darkness. But it is not mere emotion; the problem is not on this level at all. These men are not producing an art for art's sake, or emotion for emotion's sake. These things are a strong message coming out of their own world-view.

There are many media for killing men, as men, today. They all operate in the same direction: no truth, no morality. You do not have to go to art galleries or listen to the more sophisticated music to be influenced by their message. The common media of cinema and television will do it effectively for you.

MODERN CINEMA, THE MASS MEDIA AND THE BEATLES

We usually divide cinema and television programmes into two classes—good and bad. The term 'good' as used here means 'technically good' and does not refer to morals. The 'good' pictures are the serious ones, the artistic ones; the ones with good shots. The 'bad' are simply escapist, romantic, only for entertainment. But if we examine them with care we will notice that the 'good' pictures are actually the worst pictures. The escapist film may be horrible in some ways, but the so-called 'good' pictures of recent years have almost all been developed by men holding the modern philosophy of meaninglessness. This does not imply they have ceased to be men of integrity, but it does mean that the films they produce are tools for teaching their beliefs.

Four outstanding modern film producers are Fellini and

Antonioni of Italy, Slessinger of England, and Bergman of Sweden. Of these four producers Bergman has, *in the past,* perhaps given the clearest expression of the contemporary despair. He has said that he deliberately developed the flow of his pictures, that is, the whole body of his movies rather than just individual films, in order to teach existentialism.

His existentialist films extended up to but do not include the film *The Silence.* This film is a statement of utter nihilism. Man, in this picture, does not even have the hope of authenticating himself by an act of the will. *The Silence* is a series of snapshots with immoral and pornographic themes. The camera just takes them without any comment. 'Click, click, click, cut!' That is all there is. Life is like that: unrelated, having no meaning as well as no morals.

In passing, it should be noted that Bergman's presentation in *The Silence* is related to the American 'Black Writers' (nihilistic writers), the anti-statement novel and Capote's *In Cold Blood.* These, too, are just a series of snapshots without any comment as to meaning or morals.

Such writers and directors are controlling the mass media, and so the force of the monolithic world-view of our age presses in on every side. The posters advertising Antonioni's *Blow-Up* in the London Underground were inescapable as they told the message of that film: 'Murder without guilt; Love without meaning'. The mass of people may not enter an art museum, may never read a serious book. If you were to explain the drift of modern thought to them they might not be able to understand it, but this does not mean that they are not influenced by the things they see and hear—including the cinema and what is considered as 'good', non-escapist television.

No greater illustration could be found of the way these concepts are carried to the masses than 'pop' music and especially the work of the Beatles. The Beatles have moved through several stages including the concept of the drug and psychedelic approach. The psychedelic began with their records *Revolver,*[4] *Strawberry Fields Forever,* and *Penny Lane.*[5] This was developed with great expertness in their record *Sergeant Pepper's Lonely Hearts Club Band*[6] in which psychedelic music, with open statements concerning drug-taking, is knowingly presented as a religious answer. The religious form is the same vague pantheism which predominates much of the new mystical thought today. One indeed does not have to understand in a clear way the modern monolithic thought in order to be infiltrated by it. *Sergeant Pepper's Lonely Hearts Club Band* is an ideal example of the manipulating power of the new forms of 'total art'. This concept of total art increases the infiltrating power of the message by carefully conforming the technical form used to the message involved. This is used in the Theatre of the Absurd, the Marshal McLuhan type of television programme, the new cinema, the new dance and the new music following John Cage. The Beatles use this in *Sergeant Pepper's Lonely Hearts Club Band* by making the whole record one unit so the whole is to be listened to as a unit and makes one thrust, rather than the songs being only something individually. In this record the words, the syntax, the music, and the unity of the way the individual songs are arranged, form a unity of infiltration.

CHAPTER 5

The Unifying Factor in the Steps of Despair

The line of despair is a unit and the steps in the line have a distinguishing and unifying mark. With Hegel and Kierkegaard man gave up the concept of a rational, unified field of knowledge and accepted instead the idea of a leap of faith in those areas which make man to be man—purpose, love, morals and so on. It was this leap of faith that originally caused the line of despair.

The various steps on the line—philosophy, art, music, theatre and so on—differ in details, and these details are interesting and important, but in a way they are only incidental. The distinctive mark of the twentieth century intellectual and cultural climate does not lie in the differences but in the unifying concept. This unifying concept is the concept of a divided field of knowledge.

Whether the symbols to express this are those of painting, poetry or theology, is incidental. The vital question is not the symbols used to express these ideas (for example, the words of the existential philosophers or the sounds of musique concrète), but the concept of truth and the method of attaining truth involved. *The water-shed is the new way of talking about and arriving at truth, and not the terms the individual disciplines use to express these ideas.*

Léopold Sédar Senghor (b. 1906), President of Senegal, is probably the only real intellectual who is head of a Government today, anywhere in the world. He studied in France. Senghor has written a book which consists of three political speeches given to groups in his own country. The book is called *On African Social-ism*[1]. A few months ago he very kindly sent me an autographed copy of this book. As well as this he has written some magnificent poetry which has, fortunately, been well translated into English.[2]

As I read his speeches I was much moved. If a man stood up in any of the Western countries and delivered these as political speeches, very few Christians would understand their real significance. The fact that Senghor is an African underlines the need to train our overseas missionaries in a new way, for the problem of communication in our day extends beyond the Sorbonne, Oxford, Cambridge, Harvard or the Massachusetts Institute of Technology

44

to those places which we have traditionally thought of as 'the mission-field'. The problem of communication does not end at our own shores. Amongst educated men the new way of thinking is everywhere.

Senghor shows in these speeches on African socialism that he understands the modern issues exceedingly well. He points out that the methodology affecting thought today is the same on both sides of the Iron Curtain. In his book he develops in detail the change from the classical concept of logic (A is not non-A) to the general acceptance today of Hegel's methodology of synthesis.

He says correctly that originally the Marx and Engels form of communism had an interest in man, and that gave it much of its drive. We shall note, of course, that later, as it developed naturally from its presuppositions, man became devaluated in the communist state. (The Marx–Engels form of communism is properly to be regarded as a Christian heresy. Only Christianity, of all the world's religions, has produced a real interest in man. Buddhism, Hinduism and Islam never could have produced *idealistic* communism because they do not have sufficient interest in the individual.) The one thing about communism which really caught the fancy of idealistic communists was this concern with man. But, as I have said, the source of a real care for people *as individuals* comes from biblical Christianity. Are we losing our impact? It may be due largely to a failure to communicate that we believe that man, in the presence of the God who is there, is truly wonderful. But let us return to Senghor.

In his speeches he argues that one must not think of Marxism as being primarily an economic theory. Nor must one think that its atheism is central. Atheistic it most certainly is, but that is not the crux of the system. If you want to understand what Marxism really is, says Senghor, you must remember that it rests upon the dialectic methodology.

Senghor goes on to say that he and Senegal cannot accept Marxism's economic theory completely. Neither will they accept its atheism. But they will hold fast to its method of dialectic. In doing this they will follow Teilhard de Chardin[3]. In other words, Senghor realises that there is no basic difference between the dialectical approach of Marx and that of Teilhard de Chardin.[4] He appreciates that in methodology they are both on the same side. The fact that the Jesuit priest uses the word 'god' and Marx does not makes no difference, for the word by itself is meaningless until given content. The really important thing is that they both use the dialectic methodology.

If you want to understand the century you live in you must

45

realise that it is not the outward form which the dialectic takes which is the real enemy. This may be expressed in theistic or atheistic forms. The real enemy is not the incidental form it takes, but the dialectic methodology itself.

ROMANTICISM IS DEAD: CHRISTIANITY'S OPPORTUNITY IF ANTITHESIS IS MAINTAINED

In one way a Christian ought to be glad that so many live under the line of despair and are fully aware of their position. The Christian should be thankful, that when he talks to these people he does not have to remove page after page of optimistic answers, which are against all the evidence and without any base. For Christianity is not romantic; it is realistic.

Christianity is realistic because it says that if there is no truth, there is also no hope; and there can be no truth if there is no adequate base. It is prepared to face the consequences of being proved false and say with Paul: If you find the body of Christ, the discussion is finished, let us eat and drink for tomorrow we die.[5] It leaves absolutely no room for a romantic answer. For example, in the realm of morals, Christianity does not look over this tired and burdened world and say that it is slightly flawed, a little chipped, but easily mended. Christianity is realistic and says the world is marked with evil and man is truly guilty all along the line. Christianity refuses to say that you can be hopeful for the future if you are basing your hope on evidence of change for the better in mankind. The Christian agrees with the man in real despair, that the world must be looked at realistically, whether in the area of Being or in morals.

Christianity is poles apart from any form of optimistic humanism. But it also differs from nihilism, for nihilism, though it is correctly realistic, nevertheless can give neither a proper diagnosis nor the proper treatment for its own ills. Christianity has a diagnosis and then a solid foundation for an answer. The difference between Christian realism and nihilism is not that the Christian world-view is romantic. We should be pleased that the romanticism of yesterday has been destroyed. In many ways this makes our task of presenting Christianity to modern man easier than that of our forefathers.

But to rejoice that romantic answers will no longer do, and to be glad in one sense that men like Dylan Thomas have ended by weeping, does not mean that we should not be filled with compassion for our fellow men. To live below the line of despair is not to live in paradise, whether that of a fool or any other kind. It is

46

in a real sense to have a foretaste of hell now, as well as the reality in the life to come. Many of our most sensitive people have been left absolutely naked by the destruction. Should we not grieve and cry before God for such people?

In this situation which so desperately cries out for the remedy which only biblical Christianity can give we seem to be failing. This cannot be due to lack of opportunity; already men are part way to the Gospel, for they too believe that man is *dead*, dead in the sense of being meaningless. Christianity alone gives the reason for this meaninglessness, that their revolt has separated them from God who exists, and thus gives them the true explanation of the position to which they have come. But we cannot take advantage of our opportunity, *if we let go* in either thought or practice the methodology of antithesis. That is, that A is not non-A. If a thing is true, the opposite is not true; if a thing is right, the opposite is wrong.

If our own young people within the churches and those of the world outside see us playing with the methodology of synthesis, in our teaching and evangelism, in our policies and institutions, we can never expect to take advantage of this unique moment of opportunity presented by the death of romanticism. If we let go of our sense of antithesis, we will have nothing left to say.

Moreover, not only do we have nothing to say, we become nothing. Christianity ceases to exist, though it may still keep its outward institutional form. Christianity turns upon antithesis, not as some abstract concept of truth, but in the fact that God exists, and in personal justification. The biblical concept of justification is a total, personal antithesis. Before justification, we were dead in the kingdom of darkness. The Bible says that in the moment that we accept Christ we pass from death to life. This is total antithesis at the level of the individual man. Once we begin to slip over into the other methodology—a failure to hold on to an absolute which can be known by the whole man, including what is logical and rational in him—historic Christianity is destroyed, even if it seems to keep going for a time. We may not know it, but when this occurs, the marks of death are upon it, and it will soon be one more museum piece.

To the extent that anyone gives up the mentality of antithesis, he has moved over to the other side, even if he still tries to defend orthodoxy or evangelicalism. If Christians are to take advantage of the death of romanticism, we must consciously build back the mentality of antithesis among Christians. We must do it by our teaching and by example in our attitude to compromise, both ecclesiastically and in evangelism. To fail to exhibit that we take truth seriously at those points where there is a cost in our doing so, is to push the next generation into the dialectical mill-stream that surrounds us.

Finally, and with due reverence, may I emphasise that not only should we have genuine compassion for the lost amongst whom we live, but also concern for our God. We are His people, and if we get caught up in the other methodology, we have really blasphemed, discredited and dishonoured Him, for the greatest antithesis of all is that He exists as opposed to His not existing. He is the God who is there.

The Relationship of The New Theology
to The Intellectual Climate

CHAPTER I

The Fifth Step—Theology

DEPARTURE FROM BIBLICAL CHRISTIANITY

Modern existential theology finds its origin in Kierkegaard, as does secular existentialism. They are related together at the very heart of their systems, that is, 'the leap of faith'. Theology comes as the last step, but it is by no means isolated from the rest of the cultural consensus we have been reviewing.

There is diversity within the unity of the new theology. There is a difference, for example, between neo-orthodoxy and the new liberalism following the new Heidegger. If we want to be careful scholars we must appreciate such differences. But if we miss the unity which binds together all expressions of modern theology, we have missed the essential point.

At the time of the Reformation the reformers were confronted with a total system. They did not say that there were no Christians within the Roman Catholic Church, nor did they say that there were no differences in the teaching and emphases of the various Roman Catholic Orders. But they understood that there was one underlying system which bound every part of the Church together, and it was this system *as a system* that they said was wrong and in opposition to the teaching of the Bible.

Today, evangelicals are again confronted with an overwhelming consensus, a methodology accepted by theologians on every side. Thus, while one can get some insights in detail—for example, Bultmann has some good exegesis in details—yet this is not the place for ambivalent judgment—that is, mere disagreement in details—we must realise that their system *as a system* is wrong.

As Senghor pointed out that the basic factor of Marxism was neither its economic theory nor its atheism but its dialectical methodology, so the unifying factor of the new theology is its wrong methodology. Its concept of truth is wrong and because of this, what sounds right in fact often means something entirely different from that which historic Christianity means by the same phrase. It is naïve to discuss the theological questions as theological questions until one has considered what truth means to the one who is making the theological statements.

Theology has been through the same process as philosophy, though several decades later. Prior to Hegel, rationalistic man was still trying to draw his circles to encompass the whole of life. Then came the line of despair. Naturalistic theology has followed this very closely. The old liberal theologians in Germany began by accepting the presupposition of the uniformity of natural causes as a closed system. Thus they rejected everything miraculous and supernatural, including that in the life of Jesus Christ. Having done that, they still hoped to find an historical Jesus in a rational, objective, scholarly way by separating the supernatural aspects of Jesus' life from the 'true history'.

But they failed in the same way that the rationalistic philosophers had failed. They too were caught in the round room without an exit. Their search for the historical Jesus was doomed to failure, for the supernatural was so intertwined with the rest that, if they ripped out all the supernatural, there was no Jesus left! If they removed all the supernatural no historical Jesus remained; if they kept the historical Jesus the supernatural remained as well.

After their failure, they could have done two things in order to continue in a rational and logical realm. They could have left their rationalism and returned to the biblical theology of the Reformation, which they had rejected on the basis of naturalistic presuppositions; or they could have become nihilistic concerning thought and life. But instead of choosing one of these two rational alternatives, they chose a third way, just as the philosophers had already done—a way which had been unthinkable to educated man before this, and which involved the division of the concept of truth.

Why did theology follow philosophy in this tremendously important step? For two reasons: firstly, their old optimistic rationalism had failed to produce an historically credible Jesus, once the miraculous had been rejected; secondly, since the surrounding consensus of thought which they were carefully following was normative to them, when philosophy developed in this direction, they eventually followed.

So it was not so much neo-orthodoxy which destroyed the older form of liberalism, even though Karl Barth's teaching might have been the final earthquake which shook down the tottering edifice; rather it had already been destroyed from within. To say it in another way—if Barth had spoken fifty years before, it is doubtful if any would have listened.

Neo-orthodoxy gave no new answer. What existential philosophy had already said in secular language, it now said in theological language. We can represent it like this:

THE NON-RATIONAL AND NON-LOGICAL	A crisis first-order experience. Faith as an optimistic leap without verification or communicable content.
THE RATIONAL AND LOGICAL	The Scripture full of mistakes. Pessimism.

Neo-orthodoxy leaped to what I call the 'upper storey' in order to try to find something which would give hope and meaning to life. The 'lower storey' is the position to which their presuppositions would have rationally and logically brought them.

So theology too has gone below the line of despair:

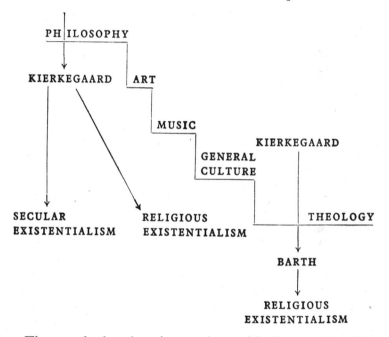

The new theology has given up hope of finding a unified field of knowledge. Hence, in contrast to biblical and Reformation theology, it is an anti-theology.

Seen in this way, it is untutored to study the new theology as if it were a subject on its own. A couple of years ago I was speaking at one of the most solidly biblical seminaries in the world. I began by saying that if our American theologians had understood the Armory Show of 1913 in New York, when modern art was first shown in the United States, perhaps the big denominations in

America would not have been captured by the liberals in the thirties. By that time, the trends which would come much later in theology were being foreshadowed in art. This is why, earlier, I gave 1913 as such an important date. Had the Christians understood the message of this art at the Armory Show, it would have been a tremendous opportunity to have been ahead rather than to have lagged behind. Conservative theology has not yet caught up. It has been far too provincial, isolated from general cultural thinking.

Karl Barth was the doorway in theology into the line of despair. He continued to hold the higher (negative) critical theories which the liberals held and yet, by a leap, sought to by-pass the two rational alternatives—a return to the historic view of Scripture or an acceptance of pessimism. After the first edition of his Epistle to the Romans, he no longer acknowledged his debt to Kierkegaard. However, still believing the higher critical theories, his 'leap' still continued to be the base of his optimistic answers. In later years as his followers have carried his views forward he has drawn back from their consistent extensions. But as Kierkegaard, with his leap, opened the door to existentialism in general, so Karl Barth opened the door to the existentialistic leap in theology. As in other disciplines, the basic issue is the shift in epistomology.

He has been followed by many more, men like Reinhold Niebuhr, Paul Tillich, Bishop John Robinson, Alan Richardson and all the new theologians. They may differ in details, but their struggle is the same—it is the struggle of modern man who has given up a unified field of knowledge. As far as the theologians are concerned, they have separated religious truth from contact with science on the one hand and history on the other. Their new system is not open to verification, it must simply be believed.

Thus, though their position rests on a 'liberal' view of Scripture, yet in the new theology the real issue is now not only their view of Scripture but their divided view of truth.

CHAPTER 2

Modern Mysticism: Despair Beyond Despair

The despair of modern man takes many forms. It is despair in depth in that it tends to use formulations and forms which seem to give hope and yet in the nature of the case lead to more profound depths of despair.

Modern nihilism is the simplest form of despair. For example, it is transparently clear in Gauguin's painting *What, Whence, Whither* and in musique concrète. Nihilism accepts the conclusion that everything is meaningless and chaotic.

The second level of despair is the acceptance of the dichotomy we have been talking about:

A blind optimistic hope of meaning, based on a non-rational leap of faith

---

The rational and the logical which gives no meaning

To feel the force of this deeper form of despair, we must keep in mind that the 'upstairs' and the 'downstairs' of this dichotomy are in two totally watertight compartments. There is *no* interchange between them. *The downstairs has no relationship to meaning: the upstairs no relationship to reason.* Rationalistic man, having given up the methodology of antithesis (if a thing is true, the opposite is not true), has been forced to a non-unified concept of knowledge, and a resultant monstrous total antithesis between rationality and meaning.

In the rational downstairs, man is only a machine. In the non-rational upstairs, he is less than a Greek 'shade'. The films *Last year in Marienbad, Juliet of the Spirits* and *Blow-Up* put this latter point with force, showing man as he is upstairs without categories.

The dichotomy was put forth as an answer to the despair of simple nihilism; but this dichotomy is really a more profound form of despair. It means that man has both divided any unified concept of knowing and also—and this is worse—divided the unity of himself, because rationality is a part of every man. The individual man cannot even communicate to himself in his thinking except

55

on the basis of antithesis. So he thinks 'I love her', or 'The blossom on that tree is beautiful', but these are a quite meaningless jumble of words unless they stand in antithesis to the fact that he dislikes her, or that the blossom is ugly. This means that in practice a man cannot totally reject the methodology of antithesis, however much his system leads him to it, unless he experiences the total alienation from himself caused by some form of mental breakdown.

Therefore those who have sponsored the modern dichotomy of reason and meaning have not been able to live with it. Jean-Paul Sartre quarrelled with Camus because he felt Camus was not being consistent to their basic presuppositions. This was true, but then neither was Sartre consistent when he signed the Algerian Manifesto. When he did this, it was not simply in order to authenticate his being by a neutral act of the will, as in the illustration of the old lady we gave earlier, because then it would have made no difference if he had done the opposite, but because he took up a deliberately moral attitude and said it was an unjust and dirty war. His left-wing political position as a moral issue is another illustration of the same inconsistency.

As far as many secular existentialists have been concerned, from the moment Sartre signed the Algerian Manifesto he was regarded as an apostate from his own position and toppled from his place of leadership of the avant-garde.

What has been true for Camus and Sartre—that they cannot live with the conclusions of their system—has been true for men on every step of the line of despair, whether in philosophy, art, music or literature. The result of not being able to stand in the honest integrity of their despair on either level (that of *nihilism* or that of a *total dichotomy* between reason and meaninglessness) has led to modern thought being shifted yet one stage further into a *third* level of despair, a level of mysticism with nothing there.

THEOLOGY AND SEMANTIC MYSTICISM

Neo-orthodoxy at first glance seems to have an advantage over secular existentialism, in that it appears to have more substance in its optimistic expressions than its secular counterpart. As we have seen, one difficulty of the final experience is that no one has found a way to communicate this experience—not even to himself. But in the new theology, use is made of certain religious words which have a connotation of personality and meaning to those who hear them. Real communication is not in fact established, but an *illusion* of communication is given by employing words rich in connotations. Expressing the inexpressible existential experience in religious connotation words gives an illusion of communication.

Carl Gustav Jung (1875–1961) speaks of the collective unconscious which emerges from the race as a whole. I think he is mistaken in his thinking, especially in the evolutionary origin which he gives it. And yet there is a certain memory in a culture that *is* carried on in its language. Such a language-related memory, I would suggest, is a better explanation for what Jung calls the collective unconscious.[1]

THE USE OF WORDS AND SYMBOLS

Every word has two parts. There is the dictionary definition and there is the connotation. Words may be synonymous by definition but have completely different connotations. Therefore we find that when such a symbol as *the cross* is used, whether in writing or painting, a certain connotation stirs the mind of people brought up in a Christian culture, even if they have rejected Christianity. (Of course the use of words in this way does not only apply to the symbols of Christianity but to those of other religions as well.) So when the new theology uses such words, without definition, an illusion of meaning is given which is pragmatically useful in arousing deep motivations.

This is something beyond emotion. An *illusion of communication and content* is given so that, when a word is used in this deliberately undefined way, the hearer 'thinks' he knows what it means. The use of the word *pantheism* is a good example. Though it really speaks of something absolutely and finally impersonal, yet the *theism* part of the word causes a reaction of acceptance, since *theism* carries overtones of personality. Now suppose you were to substitute the word *pan-everything-ism* (which is what it really means). The whole reaction would be different.

It is also important to notice that the new theology has tried to draw on the prestige surrounding the use of the word *symbol* in the scientific world; but with a totally changed concept of symbol. In science the use of symbol is valuable in that it is *well defined* to at least two people, the person who uses it and at least one other. It is said that when Einstein first propounded his theory of Relativity, perhaps only three or four men in the world understood it at first sight. But he would never have written it in the form he did if at least these three or four had not been able to understand it as a well defined communication of content. So the scientific symbol has become an important tool for writing increasingly lengthy formulae with greater accuracy. In other words, it has value according to the sharpness of its definition.

But the new theology uses the concept of symbol in exactly the opposite way. The only thing the theological and scientific uses have in common is the *word* symbol. *To the new theology, the usefulness of a symbol is in direct proportion to its obscurity.* There is connotation, as in the word *god*, but there is no definition. The secret of the strength of neo-orthodoxy is that these religious symbols with a connotation of personality give an illusion of meaning, and as a consequence it appears to be more optimistic than secular existentialism. You could not find a clearer example of this than Tillich's phrase 'God behind God'.

At first acquaintance this concept gives the feeling of spirituality. 'I do not ask for answers, I just believe.' This sounds sharply spiritual and it deceives many fine people. These are often young men and women who are not content only to repeat the phrases of the intellectual or spiritual *status quo*. They have become rightly dissatisfied with a dull, dusty, introverted orthodoxy given only to pounding out the well-known clichés. The new theology sounds spiritual and vibrant and they are trapped. But the price they pay for what seems to be spiritual is high, for to operate in the upper storey using undefined religious terms is to fail to know and function on the level of the whole man. The answer is not to ask these people to return to the poorness of the *status quo*, but to a living orthodoxy which is concerned with the whole man, including the rational and the intellectual, in his relationship to God.

Whenever men say they are looking for greater reality, we must show them at once the reality of *true* Christianity. This is real because it is concerned with the God who is there and who has spoken to us about Himself, not just the use of the symbol 'god' or 'christ' which sounds spiritual but is not. The men who merely use the symbol ought to be pessimists, for the mere *word* god or the *idea* god is not a sufficient base for the optimism they display.

Speaking rationally, the new theologians are in the same position as Pierre Schaeffer with his musique concrète. But it is as though they were asking us by a leap of faith to hear musique concrète as if it were the same as the unity and diversity of J. S. Bach. This is the kind of 'believism' which is demanded by this theology. *The optimistic jump is a necessity because man is still created in the image of God, whatever he may say about himself, and as such he cannot go on living in meaninglessness.* The jump of the new theology is on the basis of religious and therefore personal terms which give the connotation of personality, meaning and communication. It is no more than a jump into an undefinable, irrational, semantic mysticism.

Even here the new theology is not unique. There are many

secular parallels for this use of the stratagem of connotation words to try to alleviate the despair caused by the loss of a rational meaning and purpose. We will now look at some examples in the different disciplines.

THE ORIGINS OF SEMANTIC MYSTICISM—LEONARDO DA VINCI

The best way to understand how modern man has been forced, often against his natural inclination, into these various levels of despair, which he has tried to alleviate by the use of loaded connotation words in the upper storey, is by looking at one of the most brilliant men of the Renaissance, Leonardo da Vinci (1452–1519).

Leonardo died as the Reformation was beginning. Francis I, king of France, who took him to France where he died, was the king to whom John Calvin addressed his *Institutes*. As a Renaissance humanist Leonardo gave an answer to life which was in complete contrast to that which the reformers were giving.

The Reformation gave rise to a definite culture, particularly in Northern Europe, and the humanism of the Renaissance (of which Leonardo was a spokesman) ultimately gave rise to the despair of modern man which is now destroying that culture. Listen to what Giovanni Gentile, known, until his fairly recent death, as Italy's greatest modern philosopher, has to say about Leonardo:

> The unity of the inward illuminates the fantasy; and the intellect comes to break up this unity into the endless multiplicity of sensible appearances. Hence the anguish and the innermost tragedy of this universal man, divided between his irreconcilable worlds, leaves in the mind an infinite longing, made up as it were of regret and sadness. It is the longing for a Leonardo different from the Leonardo that he was, one who could have gathered himself up at each phase and remained, closed himself off either altogether in his fantasy or altogether in his intelligence.[2]

What Gentile is saying is this—that Leonardo as the first real mathematician in the modern sense really understood the problem with which modern man is now grappling. He understood that, if man starts with himself alone and logically and rationally moves through mathematics, he never comes to a universal, only to particulars and mechanics. The problem can be formulated thus: how can finite man produce a unity which will cover these particulars? And if he cannot, how can these particulars have unity and meaning for him?

59

Leonardo was a neo-Platonist, who followed Ficino, and he tried to resolve the dilemma on his canvas by painting the soul. The use of the word soul here does not mean the Christian idea of soul, but the universal. Thus, for example, he thought he could, as a painter, sketch the universal baby which would cover the particulars for all babies. But he never achieved it, any more than did Picasso in painting his abstractions. But there is a strong difference between these two. Leonardo was not a modern man and therefore could not accept Picasso's irrational solution. So Leonardo died in despondency, for he would never let go of his hope of finding a unified field of knowledge which included both the universal and the particular; both mathematics and meaning. Had he been willing to accept an irrational dichotomy, as have men following Kierkegaard, he could have been at ease. But for him this would have been an impossible answer; men of his day, humanists though they may have been, would never have accepted such an irrational solution.

So there is an unbroken line from the humanism of the Renaissance to the modern philosophy, but in the process modern man accepted the 'leap' which philosophers of the past would never have accepted, and have moved into three areas of despair: (1) Simple nihilism; (2) the acceptance of the absolute dichotomy; (3) a semantic mysticism based on connotation words.

This new mysticism does not expect to find a unified field of knowledge. It has firmly concluded that the awful contradictory situation whereby meaning and true rationality (the upper and lower storey) are irrevocably separated, is intrinsic to the nature of the universe. On the other hand, the old romanticism never gave up the search to find a rational unity between the upper and lower storey. This is the fundamental difference between them.

NATURE AND GRACE

This difference exists between the new mysticism and the old formulation of nature and grace.

After Thomas Aquinas (1227–74), men spent much time in seeking the relationship and possible unity of nature and grace. Before him the emphasis of the Byzantine thinkers was all on heavenly things whilst after him nature also became important as a result of Aquinas' emphasis on Aristotle. This was given expression in the painting of Cimabue (1240–1302) and Giotto (1267–1337) and in the poetry of Dante (1265–1321), Boccaccio (1313–75) and Petrarch (1304–74). By the time the full

Renaissance had flooded Europe, nature had all but overwhelmed grace. We can represent their thought in this way:

GRACE, the higher : God the creator; heaven and heavenly things, the unseen and its influence on the earth; man's soul; unity.

NATURE, the lower : The created; earth and earthly things; the visible and what it (nature+man) does on earth; man's body; diversity.

At first glance this might seem to be the same as the modern dichotomy:

THE NON-RATIONAL AND NON-LOGICAL

THE RATIONAL AND LOGICAL

But the difference between these two concepts is so absolute as to be qualitative, rather than quantitative.

The struggle concerning *nature and grace* was the struggle to find a meaning for these together, and philosophers always hoped for a unity between the two on the basis of reason. (In passing, one must add that this question of nature and grace can only be solved by the full biblical system, and it was because these men tried to find a rationalistic or humanistic answer that they failed.) But modern man has given up all hope of finding a unified answer to the question of nature and grace. Therefore he describes it differently and the difference of his formulation indicates his despair.[3] Modern man now formulates it like this:

Contentless faith (no rationality)

Rationality (no meaning)

To understand this at a profound level is to comprehend how completely modern man's despair *is* despair. All the new theology and mysticism is nothing more than a faith contrary to rationality, deprived of content and incapable of communication. You can bear 'witness' to it but you cannot discuss it. Rationality and faith are totally out of contact with each other.

Let us now change the horizontal line into a *line of anthropology*. Below this line is the area of man. All that the new theology has above this line is the 'philosophic other', a metaphysical infinite, which is unknown and unknowable. Like this:

god equals the Philosophic Other, unknown and unknowable

the word god undefined

The new theology is totally below the line of anthropology. It

61

knows nothing of man being created in the image of God, nor of God revealing Himself truly in the Scriptures.

The important thing is that, though nothing can be known above the line, yet nevertheless they go on using the word god.

Probably the best way to describe this concept of modern theology is to say that it is faith in faith, rather than faith directed to an object which is actually there. A year or so ago I spoke at the University of Freiburg in Germany on the topic, 'Faith *v.* faith', speaking on the contrast between Christian faith and modern faith. It is the same word but has an opposite meaning, for a modern man cannot talk about the object of his faith, only about the faith itself. So he can discuss the existence of his faith and its 'size' as it exists against all reason, but that is all. Modern man's faith turns inward.

In Christianity the value of faith depends upon the object towards which the faith is directed. So it looks outward to the God who is there, and the Christ who in history died upon the cross once for all, finished the work of atonement and on the third day rose again in space and in time. This makes Christian faith open to discussion and verification.[4]

On the other hand the new theology is in a position where faith is introverted, because it has no certain object, and where the preaching of the Kerygma is infallible since it is rationally not open to discussion. This position, I would suggest, is actually a greater despair and darkness than the position of those modern men who commit suicide.

CHAPTER 3

Modern Mysticism in Action: Art and Language

THE TENSION OF BEING MAN

There is a real tension in being a modern man because no man can live at ease in the area of despair. A Christian knows that this is because man has been made in the image of God and, though man is fallen, separated from God by his true guilt, yet nevertheless he has not become a machine. The fallenness of man does not lead to *machineness*, but to *fallen-manness*. Therefore, when people feel this utter despair, there is a titanic pressure, almost like being extruded (though it is against all the long history of reasoned thinking) to accept a dichotomy, and then later to accept some mysticism which gives an illusion of unity to the whole.

I remember sitting in Lyons' Corner House near Marble Arch in London a couple of years ago, talking to a brilliant young physicist. I asked him about the latest work he was doing and he told me about a new idea that he thought might solve Einstein's problem concerning electromagnetism and gravity. He got very enthusiastic about this, because I knew enough about the subject to stimulate him, and he was far away in his thought. Then I brought him back by saying, 'This is fine for the Christian, who really knows who he is, to say that the material universe may finally be reduced to energy particles moving in opposite directions in a vortex, but what about your naturalistic colleagues? What happens to them when they go home to their wives and families at night?'

He paused for a moment and then said, 'Oh, Dr. Schaeffer, they just have to live in a dichotomy.'

The very 'mannishness' of man refuses to live in the logic of the position to which his humanism and rationalism has brought him. To say that I am only a machine is one thing, to live consistently as if this were true is quite another.

Again I remember one night crossing the Mediterranean on the way from Lisbon to Genoa. It was a beautiful night. On board the boat I encountered a young man who was building radio stations in North Africa and Europe for a big American company.

He was an atheist, and when he found out I was a pastor he anti-
cipated an evening's entertainment, so he started in. But it did not
go quite that way. Our conversation showed me that he understood
the implications of his position and tried to be consistent concerning them. After about an hour I saw that he wanted to draw the
discussion to a close, so I made one last point which I hoped he
would never forget, not because I hated him, but because I cared
for him as a fellow human being. I noticed that he had his lovely
little Jewish wife with him. She was very beautiful and full of life
and it was easy to see, by the attention he paid her, that he really
loved her.

Just as they were about to go to their cabin, in the romantic
setting of the boat sailing across the Mediterranean and a beautiful
full moon shining outside, I finally said to him, 'When you take
your wife into your arms at night, can you be sure she is there?'

I hated to do it to him, but I did it knowing that he was a man
who would really understand the implications of the question and
not forget. His eyes turned, like a fox caught in a trap, and he
shouted at me, 'No, I am not always sure she is there', and walked
into his cabin. I am sure I spoiled his last night on the Mediterranean and I was sorry to do so. But I just pray that as long as
he lives he will never forget that, when his system was placed
against biblical Christianity, it could not stand, not on some
abstract point, but at the central point of *his own humanity*, in love.

In a different, but related way this is also true of a man like
Bernard Berenson (1865–1959). He was the world's greatest expert
on Renaissance art during his lifetime. He graduated from
Harvard, and lived most of his later life in Florence. He was such
an authority on his subject, that when he dated and priced a picture
it was generally accepted as decisive. He was a truly 'modern' man
and accepted sexual amorality. Therefore, when he took Mary
Costelloe (sister of the American essayist Logan Pearsall Smith)
away from her husband, he lived with her for a number of years
until her husband died and then married her (the Costelloes'
marriage was Roman Catholic and so a divorce could not be
arranged). When Berenson eventually married her, they had an
agreement that they would both be free to engage in extra-marital
love affairs, and both took advantage of the agreement many times.
They lived this way for forty-five years. When anyone chided
Berenson he would simply say, 'You are forgetting the animal basis
of our nature.' Thus he was perfectly willing in his private life to
accept a completely animal situation.

But in contrast to this, he expressed a completely different view
where his real love and true integration point—Renaissance art—

64

was concerned. 'Bernard Berenson found that modern figure painting in general was not based on seeing, on observing, but on exasperation and on the preconceived assumption that the squalid, the sordid, the violent, the bestial, the misshapen, in short . . . low life was the only reality!'¹ In the area of sexual morals he was perfectly willing to live consistently to his view of life as an animal. But in the area which became his attempt to find an integration point, that of art, he was prepared to say that he disliked modern art *because it is bestial!* No man like Berenson can live with his system. Every truly modern man is forced to accept some sort of leap in theory or practice, because the pressure of his own humanity demands it. He can say what he will concerning what he himself is, but no matter what he says he is, he still is man.

These kinds of leaps, produced in desperation as an act of blind faith, are totally different from the faith of historic Christianity. On the basis of biblical Christianity a rational discussion and consideration can take place, because it is fixed in the stuff of history. When Paul was asked whether Jesus was raised from the dead, he gave a completely non-religious answer, in the twentieth-century sense. He said: 'There are almost five hundred living witnesses; go and ask them!'² This is the faith that covers the whole man, including his reason; it does not ask for a belief into the void. As the twentieth-century mentality would understand the concept of religion, the Bible is a non-religious book.

MYSTICISM IN ART—PAUL KLEE AND SALVADOR DALI

In one of his writings Paul Klee (1879–1940) speaks of some of his paintings as though they were a kind of artistic ouija board. (An ouija board is a little board used by spiritists upon which participants place their hands and then ask questions. The spirits are supposed to move the board and spell out the answers.)

Paul Klee and men like him use art like a ouija board; not because they believe there are any spirits there to speak, but because they hope that the universe will push through and cause a kind of automatic writing, this time in painting. It is an automatic writing with no one there, as far as anyone knows, but the hope is that the 'universe' will speak.

Klee not only painted and drew but also wrote about his work in an attempt to explain what he was doing. In his essay *Creative confession*³ he has this to say: 'People used to reproduce things seen on earth—things which had been or would be seen with pleasure.

Today the reality of visible objects has been revealed and the belief has been expressed that, in relation to the universe, the visible is only an isolated case and that other truths exist latently and are in the majority.' He goes on to employ a phrase 'plastic polyphony', which means 'elements and their regrouping'. To Klee the word 'elements' is a technical term which he defined in his essay as 'points, the energy of the line, surface and space'. He is referring to these as he continues: 'But that [the elements] is not art in its most exalted form. In its most exalted form there is behind the ambiguity a last mystery and at that point the light of the intellect dies away miserably.' So he too allows himself to be placed in the dichotomy. He hopes that somehow art will find a meaning, not because there is a spirit there to guide the hand, but that through it the universe will speak though it is impersonal in its basic structure.

I would add that in almost all forms of the new mysticism there is a growing acceptance of the ideas of pantheism. The West and the East are coming together, and these pantheistic concepts are one of the strongest elements in the semantic mysticism of which we are speaking.

In his earlier days Salvador Dali (b. 1901) was a surrealist. As such he united the teaching of Dada with the concept of the Freudian unconscious, because this is what surrealism is. But at a certain point he could stand this no longer, and so he changed.

One day he painted his wife and called the picture, *The Basket of Bread*. It is obvious from looking at the picture that on that day he really loved her. It is the same kind of situation which came about when Picasso wrote on his canvas 'I love Eva'. Before I had heard of any change in Dali, I saw a reproduction of this picture and it was obvious that there was something different being produced. It is significant that his wife has kept this painting in her private collection.[4]

So on this particular day Dali gave up his surrealism and began his new series of mystical paintings. He had, in fact, already painted two other pictures, both called *A Basket of Bread*, one in 1926 and one in 1945, which just showed baskets of coarse Spanish bread. But this third picture, also painted in 1945, was of his wife Galarina, and shows her with one breast exposed. Her name is written on the picture, and the wedding ring is prominent on her finger.

The second painting in his new style was called *Christ of Saint John of the Cross*, painted in 1951, which now hangs in the Glasgow Art Gallery. Salvador Dali has written about this painting in a little folder on sale in the museum: 'In artistic texture and technique I painted the *Christ of Saint John of the Cross* in the manner in which I had already painted my *Basket of Bread*, which even then, more or less unconsciously, represented the Eucharist to me.'

What does he mean? He means that, when he looks at his wife one day, really loving her, and paints her with one breast exposed, this is equated by him to the eucharist; not in the sense that anything really happens, either in the Roman Catholic concept of the Mass, or that anything really happened back there in Palestine, two thousand years ago, but his love jarred him into a modern type of mysticism.[5]

In this painting he differed from Picasso with his *J'aime Eva*. Picasso never really went beyond the problems of his individual loves, but to Dali it became the key to a mysticism. In order to express the leap that he felt forced to take, he picked up Christian symbols, not to express Christian concepts, but a non-rational mysticism.

After these two paintings he painted his next Crucifixion, called *Corpus Hyperoubus*, which now hangs in the Metropolitan Museum of Art in New York, and then later he painted his *The Sacrament of the Last Supper*, which is in the National Gallery of Art in Washington. This latter painting expresses his thought vividly. As the viewer looks at Jesus he can see the background showing through him; he is a mist. This is no Christ of history. Above him stands a great human figure with arms outspread, its head cut off by the top edge of the picture. No one is sure what this figure is. However, it is strongly reminiscent of the 'Yaksa' which in Hindu art and architecture often stands behind the 'saviours' ('saviour' here bearing no relation to the Christian idea). Yaksa and Yaksi connect vegetable life with man on one side and the complete concept of pantheism on the other. I *think* this is what Dali is also saying by this cut-off figure in the painting. Whether this is so or not, the symbolism of the form of the 'room' is clear because it is constructed by means of the ancient Greek symbol of the universe.

In an interview Dali connects this religious interest of his later life with science's reduction of matter to energy: 'The discoveries in Quantum physics of the nature of energy, that matter becomes energy, a state of dematerialisation. I realised that science is moving toward a spiritual state. It is absolutely astonishing, the mystical approach of the most eminent scientists: the declarations of Max Planck and the views of Pierre Teilhard de Chardin, a great Jesuit scientist: that man in his constant evolution is coming closer and closer to a oneness with God.'

Here he relates his own mysticism and the religious mysticism of Teilhard de Chardin to impersonal dematerialisation rather than to anything personal. He is quite correct and need not have confined himself to progressive Roman Catholicism, but could also have included the Protestant forms of the new theology.

It is perfectly possible to pick up non-defined Christian symbols or words and use them in this new mysticism, though giving them opposite meanings. Their use does not necessarily imply that they have Christian meanings. Dali's secular mysticism, like the new theology, gives the philosophic other or impersonal 'everything' a personal name in order to get relief from meaninglessness by connotation.

MYSTICISM IN LANGUAGE—HEIDEGGER

Because he could not live with his existentialism Heidegger as an older man moved his position. His new position rests on these points: (1) Something, *Being*, is there; (2) This something makes itself known; (3) Language is one with Being and makes Being known. We can never know rationally about what is there (brute fact), but language does reveal that something is there. Thus language is already itself an interpretation (a hermeneutic).

He postulates that there was long ago an era, before Aristotle and the entrance of rationality, when men spoke in Greek in such a way that the universe was speaking ideally. He then tries to transfer this to all of man's language—not the content of what is spoken, but simply the flow of language. In this way the existence of language becomes for Heidegger the mysticism by which he tries to find relief from his previous existential dichotomy. It is semantic mysticism because it does not deal with content in language but simply language as such. Man speaking becomes the mouthpiece of the impersonal 'What is' (Being). The impersonal and unknown Being speaks through the being who speaks (verbalises), that is, man.

This could be a quite correct view if there were any personality behind man who really could speak meaningfully to and through man. But because Heidegger is a rationalist and begins absolutely from himself, he cannot accept that a person behind man has spoken. So he is shut up to his form of semantic mysticism. The word 'language' is a connotation word which seems to involve personality. This whole solution hangs on the connotation inherent in the one word 'language'.

At the end of his book *What is Philosophy?*[26] he says that in our modern day this use of language is found particularly in the poet. So the conclusion of this view is that we are to listen to the poet.

This does not mean we are to listen to the *content* of what the poet says, but to listen to the fact that *there is a speaking which exists.* That is all.

There is a strong parallel between Klee and Heidegger here. Both speak of their hope that somehow the universe will speak either through art or language. However, Heidegger has much more importance because by using connotation words he has become the father of a new form of the new theology—the new liberalism. There is no real difference between Heidegger's secular mysticism and the mysticism of the new theology.

CHAPTER 4

Modern Mysticism in Action: Music and Literature

MYSTICISM IN MUSIC—LEONARD BERNSTEIN AND JOHN CAGE

Leonard Bernstein's Third Symphony, which he has recorded with
the New York Philharmonic Orchestra, gives an example of the
same kind of mysticism in music. It is called the Kaddish
Symphony (1963).[1] The Kaddish is a Jewish form of music, a
Hebrew paean to God. This form Bernstein (b. 1918) has
absorbed into his modern unbelief. Now in contrast to the original
Kaddish, this one indicates that we can know nothing of what is
there, but can only listen to the musician, for he will make something of god for us. In this modern Kaddish, the concert hall is 'the
sacred house', and in it the artist will 'continue to create you,
Father, and you, me'. Art is seen as the one surviving miracle god
has left.

The reviewer Leonard Marcis in an early 1965 issue of *High
Fidelity Magazine* rightly concludes his review in this way:
'Theologians have always had artists to bridge the gap to their
flock. Now, for better or worse, the antitheologian has a powerful,
artistic statement.' Marcis correctly brings together the new secular
mysticism and the new theology. There is no certainty that there
is a god there, but the poet, musician, art as art, is the prophet
where there is no certainty about anything.

We should love good art. But art as art does not have the right
to speak *ex cathedra* regardless of content.

There was a very interesting Profile of John Cage (b. 1912) in
The New Yorker,[2] part of which we shall quote in considering his
music. The Profile says: '. . . what he is proposing is, essentially,
the complete overthrow of the most basic assumptions of Western
art since the Renaissance.' We have already seen that the young
person caught in the modern generation is four hundred years away
from the previous generation. So Cage is seeking to overthrow a
total concept stretching right back at least through those four
hundred years to the Renaissance. The article goes on to say what
it is he is smashing:

The power of art to communicate ideas and emotions, to organise life into meaningful patterns, and to realise universal truths through the self-expressed individuality of the artist are only three of the assumptions that Cage challenges. In place of a self-expressive art created by the imagination, tastes, and desires of the artist, Cage proposes an art, born of chance and indeterminacy.

If God exists and we are made in His image we can have real meaning, and we can have real knowledge through what He has communicated to us. If this is taken away we are left only with man and his finite self-expression. At this point all one has is the expression of the individual man. But Cage quite logically sees that this will not do, and so he carries man's dilemma further, smashes self-expression and leaves chance speaking. This is the basis of his music. The article continues:

A number of painters, writers, and composers in various countries have been moving in roughly the same direction in recent years, and many of them have used chance methods as a means to that end.

It names the Frenchman, Pierre Boulez, and the American, Jackson Pollock. In the last stage of his painting Jackson Pollock (1912–1956) put his canvases horizontally on the floor and dripped paint on them by chance. After doing this for some time he felt he had exhausted the chance method. This left him no way to go on further, so he committed suicide. The article continues:

Painters like the late Jackson Pollock in America and Georges Mathieu, in France, whose goal was and is certainly not anonymity, have nevertheless sought in the accidents of throwing or dripping paint a key to creation beyond the reach of the artist's conscious mind and will.

In other words, this is not merely self-expression, it is in the same direction as Paul Klee's art—the hope that through the art form the impersonal universe will somehow speak as the artist works. Further on the *New Yorker* Profile continued:

Then just as he was beginning to feel ready to stop what he called 'window-shopping' among the world's philosophies and religions, he discovered Zen-Buddhism. Dr. Daisetz T. Susiki, the first important spokesman for Zen in the West, had recently come to America and was giving weekly lectures at Columbia University that were attended by psychoanalysts, scientists, painters, sculptors, and philosophy students. They were also attended by Cage . . . By a rare coincidence, Cage found this Oriental idea perfectly summed up in the words of the seventeenth-century English music commentator Thomas Mace, who once wrote that the function of music was 'to sober and quiet the mind, thus rendering it susceptible to divine influences.'

However, it is important to note that when Mace wrote this in the seventeenth century he had the idea not only that music would quieten the mind, but that afterwards the personal God could speak to it. God was really speaking. Cage, on the other hand, has come to the point where there is nobody there to speak to him. This is the fundamental distinction. Notice how clearly this comes across in a later section of the article:

One day, young Wolff brought a copy of an ancient Chinese book—the 'I Ching' or 'Book of Changes', which Pantheon had just published in an English translation. 'The moment I opened the book and saw the charts and the hexagrams that were used for obtaining oracles according to the tossing of coins or yarrow sticks, I saw a connection with the charts I had been using', Cage says. 'It was immediately apparent to me that I could derive a means of composing from these operations, and right then and there I sketched out the whole procedure for my 'Music of Changes', which took its title from the book. I ran over to show the plan to Morty Feldman, who had rented a studio in the same building, and I can still remember him saying, 'You've hit it.'

Back in the Chinese culture long ago the Chinese had worked out a system of tossing coins or yarrow sticks by means of which the spirits would speak. The complicated method which they developed made sure that the person doing the tossing could not allow his own personality to intervene. Self-expression was eliminated so that the spirits could speak.

Cage picks up this same system and uses it. He too seeks to get rid of any individual expression in his music. But there is a very great difference. As far as Cage is concerned there is nobody there to speak. There is only an impersonal universe speaking through blind chance.

Cage began to compose his music through the tossing of coins. It is said that for some of his pieces lasting only twenty minutes he has tossed the coin thousands of times. This is pure chance, but apparently not pure enough; he wanted still more chance. So he devised a mechanical conductor. It was a machine working on cams, the motion of which cannot be determined ahead of time, and the musicians just followed this. Or as an alternative to this, sometimes he employed two conductors who could not see each other, both conducting simultaneously; anything, in fact, to produce pure chance. But in Cage's universe nothing comes through in the music except noise and confusion or total silence. All this is below the line of anthropology. Above the line there is nothing personal, only the philosophic other, or the impersonal everything.

There is a story that once, after the musicians had played Cage's total chance music, as he was bowing to acknowledge the applause, there was a noise behind him. He thought it sounded like steam escaping from somewhere, but then to his dismay realised it was the musicians behind him who were hissing. Often his works have been booed. However, when the audience boo at him they are, if they are modern men, in reality booing the logical conclusion of their own position as it strikes their ears in music.

Cage himself, however, even though he continues to compose such chance music, is another example of a man who cannot live with his own conclusions. He says that the truth about the universe is a totally chance situation. You must just live with it and listen to it; cry if you must, swear if you must, but listen and go on listening.

Towards the end of the *New Yorker* Profile we read this:

In 1954 . . . the sculptor David Weinrib and his wife moved into an old farmhouse on a tract of land in Stony Point, Rockland County, forty miles from New York, which the Williamses had bought. Cage lived and worked in an attic room that he shared with a colony of wasps, and often took long, solitary walks in the woods. His eye was caught right away by the mushrooms that grew so abundantly in Rockland County, in all shapes, and sizes and brilliant colours. He started to collect books on mushrooms and to learn everything he could about them, and he has been doing so ever since. After all, mushroom hunting is a decidedly chancy, or indeterminate pastime.

No matter how much mycology one knows—and Cage is now one of the best amateur mycologists in the country, with one of the most extensive private libraries ever compiled on the subject—there is always the possibility of a mistake in identification. 'I became aware that if I approached mushrooms in the spirit of my chance operations, I would die shortly', Cage said not long ago. 'So I decided that I would not approach them in this way!'

In other words, here is a man who is trying to teach the world what the universe intrinsically is and what the real philosophy of life is, and yet he cannot even apply it to picking mushrooms. If he were to go out into the woods and begin picking mushrooms by chance, within a couple of days there would be no Cage!

We have said before that the ideas of modern man are destroying what man is in himself. But not only that, their views cut right across what the existence of the form and structure of the external universe would indicate as well. As we see in the dilemma of Cage and his mushrooms, they cannot live on the basis of a consistent application of their views in regard to the universe, any more than they can in regard to man.

However, while Cage is forced into a hopeless dichotomy with his mushrooms, with his music he has continued to live consistently with his position, even though his music is nothing more than noise or silence. He has resisted the pressure to dress up impersonal Being in connotation words or sounds. Most modern men have not had this much courage[3].

MYSTICISM IN LITERATURE—HENRY MILLER

In the writing of his earlier books, Miller has not just set forth something which is dirty in a trivial sense, but he has succeeded in murdering everything which is meaningful, including sexual things. In these books he expressed his anti-law position, in every sense. However, Miller is another man who could not stand by his own position. Many others have been destroyed in their inner lives by his books, but he has not been able to be so tough-fibred. So he joins the growing list of modern men who have accepted the new mysticism. Miller now holds to a pantheistic view of the world.

His new views are very cogently and consistently put in the preface which he wrote to the new French edition of Elie Favre's *History of Art*. He calls his preface, *A Sense of Wonder*.[4] This is an important title, for it implies that he is going to contrast the 'sense of wonder' with the intellect. And this in fact is what he does. For example, he says, 'Above all, he [Elie Favre] was a devout worshipper of the creative spirit in man. His approach, like our own Walt Whitman's, was nothing less than cosmic.' This already has a pantheistic ring about it. Later on he continues, 'What impact his work may have today, particularly on the young who are almost immune to wonder and mystery because of all the knowledge which has been crammed into their heads, I do not know.' This is a significant sentence because he has set the intellect and knowledge against the sense of wonder. One's intellect would lead one only to the lower storey of rationality and logic and there there is no meaning in life, only machines. But in contrast to this one has a sense of wonder which by-passes the rational, and this sense is very much related to the use of the word *awe* that is so much in vogue today. The intellect is divorced and rejected.

A swift glance at Miller's introduction might lead the reader to think that he had suddenly become a Christian. He uses words and phrases which sound so correct. Thus, 'In investing himself (man) with the powers of a god, man has divorced himself from God — and from the universe as well. That which was his inheritance, his gift and salvation, he has vitiated through pride and arrogance of intellect. He has not only turned his back on the source, he is no longer aware that there is a source, the source from which, as the Good Book says, all blessings flow.'

It sounds most credible, and there is more to come, 'The spirit which first breathed upon the waters will create anew . . . There is no last word, unless it be the Word itself: "In the beginning was the Word, and the Word was with God, and the Word was God".' We are forced on the basis of this to ask, 'Is Henry Miller one of us ?' And the answer, which is negative, can be gleaned from a full reading of what he has said in this preface.

He says, 'It forces me, the knowledge of this truth, to observe as I have again and again that behind all creation, whether human or divine, lies an impenetrable mystery. All those epoch making names which he [Favre] reels off in his works, devastating forces when one thinks on it, because forces for good and evil simultaneously, all bear witness to the inexhaustible energy which invests even the tiniest particle of matter and demonstrate in miraculous everyday fashion that what is called matter or substance is but the adumbration of a luminous reality too powerful for our feeble senses to apprehend.' There is a strong connection here with what Salvador Dali says concerning the dematerialising of the universe.

A little further on he writes, 'It is only embryonic man to be sure who is staging this drama of annihilation.[5] The true self is indestructible.' You may think that he is referring to the individual soul here, but it is not so. He continues, 'Art more than religion offers us the clue to life', and at the beginning of the preface, 'Did he [Walt Whitman] not say somewhere that religions are born from art and not vice-versa ?' We can link this statement with what Heidegger says about the poet, *just listen* to the poet. Miller tells

75

us to look at art and not to worry about the content; art as art is the new prophet. 'Art more than religion offers us the clue to life, but only to those who practise it, those who dedicate themselves, and who come ultimately to realise that they are but the humble instruments whose privilege it is to unveil the glory and the splendour of life.' Rationality brings one to the content of Miller's books, *The Tropic of Cancer* and *The Tropic of Capricorn* and the rest. Therefore the intellect and knowledge must be put aside, and a leap made into contentless mysticism and awe.

But the man who has arrived at this point does not really matter anyway. 'What matters, in the ultimate, if for a few aeons of time this creature called man remains in abeyance, absent from the scene?' In other words, go ahead and drop the bomb, what does it matter?

The usual way of thinking, as exhibited by the shock shown following the publication of Nevil Shute's book, *On the Beach*, would be: if everybody is going to be annihilated tomorrow what is the use of writing a poem, or making a painting today? But Henry Miller and his new pantheistic mysticism would claim that it would not matter if tomorrow the oceans were calm and there were no man on the shore. *Individual* man does not matter.

However, he goes on to say, 'This is an end, one of many—not *the* end. What man is in essence can never be destroyed. The spirit which first breathed upon the waters will create anew.' He is not speaking of a personal God. He is using these connotation words to speak of pantheistic cycles. Everything, including human history, is being viewed as a series of cycles. What happens to the individuals does not matter, the cycles roll on! This is a thorough-going pantheistic idea. The man who can never be destroyed is not individual man, but just Man springing from the universe of what is. 'Man, this embryonic form of a being which has neither beginning nor end, will give way to man again. Present day man, the man of history, need not and will not be the last word. There is no last word, unless it is the Word itself. "In the beginning was the Word, and the Word was with God, and the Word was God."'

To Miller, the world can only be conceived of in pantheistic terms, in endless cycles which repeat themselves. But in order to give it a personal sound, he uses biblical terms and phrases. In this way he utilises the connotation attached to these forms, which comes out of the history of our race, to heighten the feeling of the semantic mysticism he has accepted.

The introduction is concluded with these words, 'Let us therefore, in reviewing this vast panorama of human achievement, think less of what was accomplished by the giants who parade throughout these volumes and more of the imperishable energy of which they were the fiery sparks. All may be lost, all forgotten, if only we remember that nothing is lost, nothing ever forgotten. "As it was in the beginning, is now, and ever shall be: world without end."' And with this devastating blow at the individual, who counts as nothing except as a part of the energy of the universe to which he is united as a spark to the fire, Miller finishes his introduction.

It must be plain that the new Henry Miller cannot in any sense be called a Christian. He is doing the same as Salvador Dali and the new theologians are doing, namely using Christian symbols to give an illusion of meaning to an impersonal world which has no real place for man.

This is Henry Miller, the writer of *The Tropics*, who in this preface takes up basically the same position as the new theologians.

CHAPTER 5

A New Phase of Modern Theology

GOD IS DEAD—OR ALMOST SO!

It should be quite clear by this time that the mysticism of the new theology does not separate it from the intellectual climate of the second half of the twentieth century. Rather, it once more relates the new theology to the surrounding secular climate and consensus, because, as we have seen, the parallel secular semantic mysticisms are found in every one of the steps in the line of despair—philosophy, art, music, and the general culture.

The new theology itself is having an internal problem through separating the 'upstairs' and 'downstairs' into such water-tight compartments. This is its position at the moment:

Faith=No rationality, i.e. no contact with the cosmos (science) or history

---

All rationality—including scientific evidence and history

The tension is very strong because such a total antithesis between rationality and 'religious values' destroys the unity of the individual man, and he becomes divided within himself. This has given rise to a deep-seated restlessness amongst many of the modern theologians. A new attempt is being made to breach the dichotomy. This attempt takes two forms: one form is to try to find a unity of the whole on the level of the lower storey, the other on the level of the upper.

The first form has been widely publicised as the 'God is Dead' theology. These have chosen the downstairs as a place to find a unity and they have dispensed with God altogether, including the term God. When the real God-is-Dead men say God is Dead, they do not merely mean that God is being listened to very little in our modern secular world, *but that He never was.* They put their emphasis on the lower storey and seem to deny the validity of the upper storey altogether. This leaves only the word 'Jesus' *downstairs.* But we must be careful not to get caught out, for if we turn our backs for a moment these men will use the word Jesus as a banner with *upper storey* overtones. We will represent it like this:

God is dead

| God is dead | Jesus |

These men have chosen to call themselves 'Christian Atheists'. They are atheists in the classical sense of that word; and they are Christians only in the sense that they have adopted for themselves Bonhoeffer's definition of Christ, 'The man for others'. They really differ little from today's optimistic humanists.

This is fairly straight-forward; in one sense these men are no longer 'having their cake and eating it too.' They have lost all connotation words except the term 'Jesus Christ', and even this, to the extent to which they have defined it, they have ruined as a connotation word. But they are not being left quiet in their atheism. The upper storey men who still want to keep the use of the connotation words are fighting back.

In actual fact the new theology has a dead god in both the upper and lower storeys:

The new mysticism—all knowledge concerning God is dead, any concept of a personal God is dead—therefore God is dead

On the basis of rationality God is dead

A typical exponent of the upper storey mentality is Paul Tillich. When asked at Santa Barbara, shortly before he died, if he ever prayed, he said, 'No, but I meditate'. Bishop Robinson also displays the Death of God on the upper level, for he also leaves no real place for prayer as a personal communication, and though he may talk much about love, yet there is no note of loving God.

Thus in the upper storey it is not only that *man* becomes a 'shade' but the god of the new mysticism is no more than a mist which becomes only Being or Pan-everything. If we look at the theologians operating in this upper storey we may say that they are either atheists in the classical sense, or pantheists—depending on how one looks at it. Thus their god is also dead.

This vague pantheism, which we have noted in secular thinking also, creates problems for those brought up within the Christian faith. Thus Bishop Robinson insists that God is actually transcendental after all. He spoils it, however, when he goes on to say that man is transcendental too (which, fascinatingly enough, is the exact word Sir Julian Huxley is using about man) for this therefore means that transcendental really equals non-transcendental, and we are back at square one.

When the theologians and the secular men use this word, I would suggest that they mean by it the things that surprise them when they examine man, things they could not expect to find on the basis of what they believe about man's origin. Or again, it means little more than Henry Miller's sense of wonder. So when they use this word without definition, it does not thereby mean that they have escaped from the charge of pantheism.

As far as God and man are concerned, modern theology is now like this:

Non-rational Non-logical faith	=	No categories for God, all knowledge concerning God is dead. The personal God is dead. No categories for man or his meaning.
All rationality, i.e. all contacts with the cosmos (science) all contacts with history	=	God is dead and man is a machine

A QUEST BY THE UPPER STOREY MEN

This position is a high price to pay for rejecting historic Christianity, the Christianity of the Scripture and the Creeds. But instead of returning to the biblical position, they are making a further attempt to solve their difficulties apart from it. The latest move is an attempt by the upper storey men to put a toe back into history.

Karl Barth, who can be said to be the inaugurator of all this, has felt the need to try to hold back from the logical extension of his position that his followers have developed. In the last years he has spoken of an historic resurrection of Christ. It is not quite as simple as that, however; for on their presuppositions the Bible contains historical and scientific errors and thus dichotomy, a divided concept of truth, is necessarily central in their concept of 'religious truth'.

They cannot go back to the old liberalism—there can be no going back to the old quest for the historical Jesus, for it failed. However, if they give up the division of truth (*which has been their answer to the old liberalism when it failed*) then they have to face again what the older liberalism faced: on the one side nihilism (God is dead, man is dead, and meaning is dead); on the other side, the answer of the historic and Reformation Christian position which states that there is a personal God, that man is made in His image, that He has communicated to His creature by a propositional, verbalised revelation of content, and thus this is able to be considered by the whole man. Or to put it very briefly, the only way out of their dilemma is to move back to the methodology of antithesis. Until they do this, no amount of talk about a physical resurrection of Christ will touch the heart of the discussion.[1]

80

This need to get a toe back into history by the upper storey men was ably dealt with in an article in *The Listener*, April 12, 1962 by Dr. John Macquarrie, then lecturer in Systematic Theology at Glasgow University, now at Union Theological Seminary, New York. We quote a relevant part of it. The article is called, *History and the Christ of Faith*:

A NEW QUEST

It should not surprise anybody that some of Bultmann's disciples, afraid of losing themselves in a world of myth and make-believe, have turned again to the question of the historical Jesus. Gunther Bornkamm, for instance, says that 'we must look for the history in the Kerygma' and that we should not be resigned or sceptical about the historical Jesus. Does this mean that we must reopen the interminable arguments as to whether this incident or that saying took place as recorded? It cannot mean this, for the earlier quest of the historical Jesus showed that no clear answers are to be had. The new quest is intended to be different; but unfortunately there is a good deal of confusion among those who have embarked on it as to what is intended, and Bultmann himself has been severely critical of some of them. He is content to hold that our knowledge is confined to the bare fact that there was a Jesus who was crucified, and does not extend to the manner of his life or personality.

My own view is that the Christian theologian needs to assert a minimal core of factual history if the Kerygma is to present us with a way of life that is realistic and not culled from a dream world. This minimal core is not a short list of essential incidents or sayings, but simply the *assertion*[2] that at the source of the Christian religion there was an actual historical instance of the pattern of life proclaimed in the Kerygma.

Here Dr. John Macquarrie acknowledges that these theologians cannot go back to the old liberal exhaustive search for the historical Jesus, for that ended in total failure. His own solution is the *assertion* that Jesus lived such and such a life. In other words, just say it is so.

There are two main attempts being made by the upper storey theologians to get a toe back into history in order that they should not lose themselves and God 'in a world of myth and make-believe'.

Firstly, there is the use of the phrase 'God's saving acts in history', which sounds very fine. But they do not mean by this that God has in any sense literally entered our space-time world at a particular point in order to begin and complete man's salvation. They mean that God is in some way saving or redeeming *all* history, including the most grizzly acts of sin and cruelty which have been committed by individuals or groups.

Secondly, they just use the *word* history—this can take several forms. Macquarrie says that we must assert that certain events are history. The events are chosen arbitrarily and, of course, they are not open to real historical enquiry. Or else they use the Bible as a vehicle for continuous existential experiences. They say such experiences did happen back in Bible times, but the way they are expressed in the Bible has no relation to the experience. The biblical accounts are just the faulty cultural expression of that day. This way of looking at history is closely related to what the new Heidegger said about the mystique of language. These new theologians, both Protestants and some in the Roman Catholic Church, attempt therefore to manipulate biblical language as a help towards present existential experience.[3]

To these men language is always an interpretation and therefore the words of the Bible are already an interpretation of the unknowable thing which occurred. The upper storey men are left with a flood of words.

Thus neither the lower storey men nor the upper storey men are really doing very well in trying to ease the tension they are in. But we can be sure the hopeless attempts will continue, for on one hand their dichotomy is uncomfortable in the extreme; and on the other hand, they must keep it because this division of truth is the essence of the new theology.

TODAY'S OPPORTUNITY FOR THE NEW THEOLOGY

In spite of the confusion among the new theologians and in spite of the fact that they are not really saying anything unique among the secular mysticisms which surround us, yet there are reasons why this is a moment of opportunity for the new theology to take a privileged place in our culture, a place theology has not enjoyed for a long time. It may become a leader in tomorrow's affairs.

For some time society has been in danger of losing all sociological form. Men are facing a society without structure and they want to fill the void that has appeared. For a long time Reformation ideas formed the basis of North European culture, and this extended to include that of America and English-speaking Canada, etc. But today that has been destroyed by the relativism both inside and outside the churches. Hence historic Christianity is now a minority group. Even the memory of past cultural forms is becoming weak. Moreover, the structural form of Northern Europe is not the only one which is being battered to pieces. For example one can see that Marxist Russia is moving in the same direction though at a slower rate because of its totalitarian controls. That is why modern Russian artists are being prevented from speaking freely, for they are carrying the modern thinking into Russian life.

Society cannot function without form and motivation. As the old sociological forms have been swept away, new ones must be found or society breaks down altogether. Sir Julian Huxley has stepped in at this point with his suggestion that religion has a real place in modern society. But, he would contend, it must be understood that religion is always evolving and that it needs to come under the control of society.

This suggestion is not as ridiculous as it sounds, even coming from a convinced humanist, if one understands the mentality of our age. The prevailing dialectical methodology fits itself easily into religious forms. After all, Senghor has said that on the basis of dialectical thinking his country would follow Teilhard de Chardin. It is well to remember that now men think dialectically on *both* sides of the Iron Curtain.

Teilhard de Chardin, incidentally, illustrates that the progressive Roman Catholic theologians are further away from historic Reformation Christianity than classical Roman Catholicism, because they are also dialectical thinkers.

The orthodox Roman Catholic would tell me that I am bound for hell because I reject the true Church. He is dealing with a concept of absolute truth. But the new Roman Catholic who sits at my fireside says, 'You are all right, Dr. Schaeffer, because you are so sincere.' In the new Roman Catholicism such a statement usually means that the dialectical method has taken over.

Therefore we are not surprised to find that the new Heidegger has followers, such as Karl Rahner, among some of the leading progressive Roman Catholic thinkers; and others such as Hans Küng have been strongly influenced by neo-orthodoxy. It is important to note that the position on Scripture by the Vatican Council has shifted in the same direction and men such as Raymond Panikkar,[4] Dom Bede Griffiths, O.S.C.[5] and Anthony de Mello, S.J.[6] are proclaiming a synthesis between Roman Catholicism and Hinduism. Truly these men have come a long way, but it is not in the direction of biblical Christianity. Neal Ascherson, under the date line April 29, 1967, reported in a London newspaper the recent conversations at Marienbad between the Paulus Society, which follows Karl Rahner, and Roger Garaudy, chief theoretician of the French Communist Party. He showed a streak of genius when he used the heading: 'This year in Marienbad—where Marxist and Catholic meet', thus relating this dialogue to the loss of categories as it was stressed by the film *The Last Year at Marienbad*.

The time, therefore, does seem right for this new theology to give the needed sociological forms and motivations. It is true, of course, that society could look elsewhere amongst the secular mysticisms for a new evolving religion, but the new theology has some strong advantages.

Firstly, the undefined connotation words that they are using are deeply rooted in our Western culture. This is much easier and more powerful than using new and untraditional words.

Secondly, these men control almost every large denomination in Protestantism, and if the progressives in the Roman Catholic Church consolidate their position, that Church as well. This gives them the advantage of functioning within the organisational stream of the Church, and thus both its organisation and linguistic continuity is at their disposal.

Thirdly, people in our culture in general are already in process of being accustomed to accept non-defined, contentless religious words and symbols, without any rational or historical control. Such words and symbols are ready to be filled with the content of the moment. The words 'Jesus' or 'Christ' are the most ready for the manipulator. The phrase 'Jesus Christ' has become a contentless banner which can be carried in any direction for sociological purposes. In other words, because the phrase 'Jesus Christ' has been separated from true history and the content of Scripture, it can be used to trigger religiously motivated sociological actions directly contrary to the teaching of Christ. This is already in evidence, as for example in the 'new' morality being advocated by some within the Church of England today.

So there is open to the new theology the possibility of supplying society with an endless series of religiously motivated arbitrary absolutes. It is against such manipulated semantic mysticism that we do very well to prepare ourselves, our children and our spiritual children.

How Historic Christianity Differs from The New Theology

CHAPTER I

Personality or a Devilish Din

Our forefathers used the term systematic theology to express their view that Christianity is not a series of isolated religious statements, but that it has a beginning and flows on to an end. Each part relates to each other part and to the whole, and to what stands first in the system. It is perfectly possible that such a systematic understanding of Christianity can become a dead thing, but let us not despise the word systematic as if it were automatically a corpse.

Rightly understood, Christianity as a system has the answers to the three basic needs of modern man. In this it differs from the new theology, which has no adequate basis upon which to give answers which will stand up to the test of rationality and the whole of life as we must live it.

The first basic need is caused by the lack of certainty regarding the reality of individual personality. Every man is in tension until he finds a satisfactory answer to the problem of who he himself is.

The biblical Christian answer takes us back first to the very beginning of everything and states that personality is intrinsic in what is; not in the pantheistic sense of the universe being the extension of the essence of God (or what is), but that a God who is personal on the high order of Trinity created all else. Within the Trinity, before the creation of anything, there was real love and real communication.[1] Following on from this statement, the Bible states that this God who is personal created man in His own image. A personal God created all things freely in a non-determinate fashion; and man is created in a special situation—what I would call a special circle of creation. He is the image of this kind of God and so personality is intrinsic to his make-up. God is personal, and man is also personal.

It might be helpful to illustrate the situation in this way: imagine you are in the Alps and from a high vantage point you can see three parallel ranges of mountains with two valleys in between. In one valley there is a lake, but the other is dry. Suddenly you begin to witness what sometimes happens in the Alps; a lake forming in the second valley where there was none before. As you see the water rising, you may wonder what its source is. If it stops at the same level as the lake in the neighbouring valley, you may, after careful measurements, conclude that there is a possibility that the water has come from the first valley. But if your measurement shows that the level of the second lake is twenty feet higher than the first, then you can no longer consider that its source may be from the neighbouring valley and you would have to seek another explanation. Personality is like that; no one has ever thought of a way of deriving personality from non-personal sources.

Therefore, biblical Christianity has an adequate and reasonable explanation for the source and meaning of human personality. Its source is sufficient—the personal God on the high order of Trinity. Without such a source men are left with personality coming from the impersonal (plus time, plus chance).

The two alternatives are very clear cut. Either there is a personal beginning to everything or one has what the impersonal throws up by chance out of the time sequence. The fact that the second alternative may be veiled by connotation words makes no difference. The words used by Eastern pantheism; the new theological words such as Tillich's 'Ground of Being'; the secular shift from mass to energy or motion, all eventually come back to the impersonal, plus time, plus chance. If *this* is really the only answer to man's personality, then personality is no more than an illusion, a kind of sick joke which no amount of semantic juggling will alter. Only some form of mystical jump will allow us to accept that personality comes from impersonality. This was the position into which Teilhard de Chardin was forced. His answer is only a mystical answer of words.

Because these men will not accept the only explanation which can fit the facts of their own experience, they have become metaphysical magicians. No one has presented an idea, let alone demonstrated it to be feasible, to explain how the impersonal beginning, plus time, plus chance, can give personality. We are distracted by a flourish of endless words, and lo, personality has appeared out of the hat! This is the water rising above its source. No one in all the history of humanistic, rationalistic thought has found a solution. As a result, either the thinker must say man is dead, because personality is a mirage; or else he must hang his reason on a hook outside the door and cross the threshold into the leap of faith which is the new level of despair.

A man like Sir Julian Huxley has clarified the dilemma by acknowledging, though he is an atheist, that somehow or other, against all that one might expect, man functions better if he acts as though God is there. This sounds like a feasible solution for a moment, the kind of answer a computer might give if you fed the sociological data into it. God is dead, but act as if He were alive. However, a moment's reflection will show what a terrible solution this is. Ibsen, the Norwegian, put it like this: that if you take away a man's lie you take away his hope.[2] These thinkers are saying in effect that man can only function as man for an extended period of time if he acts on the assumption that a lie (that the personal God of Christianity is there) is true. You cannot find any deeper despair than this for a sensitive person. This is not an optimistic, happy, reasonable or brilliant answer. It is darkness and death.

Imagine that a universe existed which was made up only of liquids and solids, and no free gases. A fish was swimming in this universe. This fish, quite naturally, was conformed to its environment, so that it was able to go on living. But let us suppose that by blind chance, as the evolutionists would have us believe, this fish developed lungs as it continued swimming in this universe without any gases. Now this fish would no longer be able to function and fulfill its position as a fish. Would it then be higher or lower in its new state with lungs? It would be lower, for it would drown. In the same way, if man has been kicked up out of that which is only impersonal by chance, then those things that make him man—hope of purpose and significance, love, motions of morality and rationality, beauty and verbal communication—are ultimately unfulfillable and are thus meaningless. In such a situation is man higher or lower? He would then be the lowest creature on the scale. The green moss on the rock is higher than he, for it can be fulfilled in the universe which exists. But if the world is what these men say it is, then man (not only individually but as a race), being unfulfillable, is dead. In this situation man should not walk on the grass, but respect it—for it is higher than he!

THE LOGICAL END OF DENYING PERSONALITY

Recently, while I was giving a series of lectures at an American College, I received an anonymous note from one of the students. This note read: 'A question I would like you to answer on one of your broadcast talks if you could: with reference to what you have said about some artists destroying man, what should I do? I *want* to destroy too.'

This student had touched the heart of the modern predicament. The desire of many young people—whether Mods and Rockers or university rebels—to destroy is the way they state their nihilism. At the bottom there is the valid question: if all of life is meaningless, and ultimately absurd, why bother to march straight forward, why stand in the queue as though life as a whole makes sense?

The difficulty for society in handling them is that they are right, if everything is ultimately absurd, and their nihilistic conclusions are more honest than the romantic and semantic answers given by their elders.

In face of this modern nihilism, Christians are often lacking in courage. We tend to give the impression that we will hold on to the outward forms whatever happens, even if God really is not there. But the opposite ought to be true of us, so that people can see that we demand the truth of what is there and that we are not dealing merely with platitudes. In other words, it should be understood that we take this question of truth and personality so seriously that if God were not there we would be among the first of those who had the courage to step out of the queue. In so far as we show this to be our attitude, maybe the far-out ones will begin to take us seriously and listen to what we have to say. If they do not lay hold of the idea that in our integrity we would join with them in destruction or 'dropping-out', except that we know we have an adequate basis for personality and the reality of morals, then they will not and should not listen to us.

According to the tape recording of my lecture that night, my answer to the student who said that he or she wanted to destroy was: 'I would say to you tonight, that if we live in this intrinsically impersonal world, dress it up if you will with the word pantheism, either in the Eastern thought or in the new theology or if I speak of it in secular terms, if this is what I am, and all men are, with their aspirations, if this is all they are, unfulfillable products of chance, a sterile sport, then come beside me, because I wish to destroy too. If indeed these ideas are your ideas, you should stand beside such a man to destroy. If I am an artist I should wish to destroy. I should say with Karel Appel, "I do not paint, I hit". I should say with John Cage, "It is only chance"; with a resultant noise and a devilish din. But further, let us understand, in such a case, what love will mean. Love will mean facing the problem of pushing the button that destroys the human race. This is the distinction between there being a real meaning of personality that makes it reasonable to love and have compassion, a real reason to keep humanity alive; and no real meaning, and therefore a love resulting in that which should destroy. This then would be nearer to the truth of what is, and what will eventually happen, not only to the individual, but to the human race.

'This person who wrote this note understands something. In such a case I would ask him to come by my side and destroy, but I would ask him also to be honest in considering the other possibility, that all this is not so, but rather that we started with a

90

personal beginning and therefore there is intrinsic meaning to personality, my personality, and other men's personality in this universe. This is the distinction between the two positions. The things we have considered are not only theoretical things—they are things that cut down into the warp and woof of the understanding of life. We would say indeed to the man who would destroy a romantic concept·which has no base, destroy it indeed. Demand a realistic answer. Here we stand face to face with the real issue of the new theology and the whole new thought.'

This is the crux of the matter; either an intrinsically personal 'what is', in the sense of a creation by the personal God, or John Cage's devilish din!

CHAPTER 2

Verifiable Facts and Knowing

In historic Christianity a personal God creates man in His own image, and in such a case, there is nothing that would make it nonsense to consider that He would communicate to man in verbalised form. Why should He not communicate in verbalised form when He has made man a verbalising being in his thoughts as well as in communication with other men? Having created man in His own image, why should He fail to communicate to that verbalising being in such terms? The communication would then be three ways: God to man, and vice-versa; man to man; and man to himself. Someone may raise queries as to whether in fact this is the case, but, in this field of reference, it is neither a contradictory nor a nonsense statement. Such a concept would be nonsense with the presupposition of a totally closed field of cause and effect. But if you are a person who holds that cause and effect has been and is totally closed, then you need to ask whether such a view as yours really stands up to all we know.

Why should God not communicate *propositionally* to the man, the verbalising being, whom He made in such a way that we communicate propositionally to each other? Therefore in the biblical position there is the possibility of verifiable facts involved: a personal God communicating in verbalised form propositionally to man—not only concerning those things man would call in our generation 'religious truths', but also down into the areas of history and science.

God has set the revelation of the Bible in history; He did not give it (as He could have done) in the form of a theological text-book. Having set the revelation in history, what sense then would it make for God to give us a revelation in which the *history* was wrong? God has also set man in the *universe* which the Scriptures themselves say speaks of this God. What sense then would it make for God to give His revelation in a book that was wrong concerning the universe? The answer to both questions must be, 'No sense at all!'

It is plain, therefore, that from the viewpoint of the Scriptures themselves there is a unity over the whole field of knowledge. God has spoken, in a linguistic propositional form, truth concerning Himself and truth concerning man, history and the universe.

Here is an adequate basis for the unity of knowledge. The unity encompasses both the upstairs and the downstairs. This is the answer to the discussion of the unity between nature and grace and modern man's question of knowledge above and below the line of anthropology. The unity is there because God has spoken truth into all areas of our knowledge.

At the same time, one must avoid the opposite mistake of saying that because God has communicated truly concerning science, all scientific study is wasted. This is a false deduction. To say that God communicates *truly* does not mean that God communicates *exhaustively*. Even in our human relationships we never have exhaustive communication, though what we do have may be true. Thus, as far as our position in the universe is concerned, though the infinite God has said true things concerning the whole of what He has made, our knowledge is not thereby meant to be static. Created in His image, we are rational and logical and, as such, we are able to and intended to explore and discover further truth concerning creation.

God says, in effect, 'Learn of the truth that I have made in the external world.' Finite man in the external universe, being finite, has no sufficient reference point if he begins absolutely and autonomously from himself and thus needs certain knowledge. God gives us this in the Scriptures. With this in mind the scientist can understand, in their ultimate relationships, the truths that he is looking at. Thus scientific study in itself can be to the glory of God, for here man is functioning properly in the universe in which God has placed him. He is telling us what is truly there and he is adding to the store of knowledge of his fellowmen. A scientist may serve God in his science.

The new theology cannot give an adequate framework for ascertaining facts and knowledge. It cannot because it removes the possibility of communication at the only two points that can be discussed and verified, namely history and the universe. Religious truths cannot be discussed once they are divorced from the other two. Bezzant, in the book *Objections to Christian Belief*,[1] well illustrates how crucial this matter of truth is. Though Bezzant is an older type of liberal, and though the book is destructive in many ways, nevertheless he has seen this point very clearly. He has been attacking the historic Christian position, but then suddenly he swings around and trains all his guns on neo-orthodoxy.... 'When I am told that it is precisely its immunity from proof which secures the Christian proclamation from the charge of being mythological,

93

I reply that immunity from proof can "secure" nothing whatever except immunity from proof, and call nonsense by its name.' This is a tremendous sentence. At this point he has truly understood the fatal flaw of modern theology. It may dress up its position with all kinds of clothes, but it remains irrational and what it is talking about can never really be discussed, because it is no longer open to verification.

I remember hearing the Rev. Michael Green, of the London College of Divinity, say at a conference at which we were both speaking, 'Bultmann is infallible for twenty minutes each Sunday.' That is, all the new theology can do is preach and ask the people to believe or not to believe, without the exercise of reason. In this way, man becomes *less than* the fallen man of the biblical Christian position.

The historic Christian answer concerning verifiable facts and knowing turns on who God is, on who is there. The God who is there according to the Scriptures is the personal-infinite God. There is no other god like this God. It is ridiculous to say that all religions teach the same things when they disagree at the fundamental point as to what God is like. The gods of the East are infinite by definition—the definition being 'god is all that is'. This is the pan-everything-ism god. The gods of the West have tended to be personal but limited; such were the gods of the Greeks, Romans and Germans. But the God of the Bible, Old and New Testaments alike, is the infinite-personal God.

It is this God who has created various orders of creation, like this:

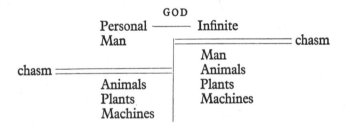

How then is God's creation related to Himself and to itself? On the side of God's infinity there is a break between God and the whole of His creation. I am as separated from God in the area of His being the Creator and infinite and I being the creature and finite, as is the atom or energy particle. I am no closer to God on this side than the machine.

However, on the side of God's *personality*, the break comes between man and the rest of creation. In terms of modern thought this is a dynamic conception of which modern man and modern theology know nothing. So Schweitzer identified himself with the hippopotamus, for he did not understand that man's relationship is upward; and therefore he looked downward to a creature which does many of the same things as himself. But on the *side of personality*, if our relationship is upward, then everything concerning man's 'mannishness' is in place.

The biblical Christian says that, on the side of personality, man can know God truly, though he cannot know God exhaustively. Unlike the new theology, he is not trapped by the two alternatives of knowing God completely or not knowing Him at all. We are not shut up to a total comprehension of the infinite.

Modern man and the new theology has only this:

Infinite

————————————— chasm

Man
Animal
Plant
Machine

Modern man has driven a wedge between the personal and the infinite and says that personality equals finiteness. He has equated personality with limitedness. But the Christian says that the only *limitation* which personality intrinsically must have is that it cannot be impersonal at the same time. To say that personality must always be limited in other ways is to try to make an absolute which one cannot make. Indeed, human personalities are limited in other ways, but this is because they are created and finite, not because they are personal. *Personality as such cannot necessarily imply limitedness.*

A man from Israel who was an atheist wrote and asked me, 'What sense does it make for a man to give his son to the ants, to be killed by the ants, in order to save the ants?' I replied that it makes no sense at all for a man to give his son to the ants, to be killed by the ants, in order to save the ants, because man *as a personality* is totally separated from the ants. Man's only relation to the ants is in the areas of Being and creaturehood. However, in the area of personality man's relationship *is* upward to God and therefore the incarnation and death of the Son of God for the sake of man's salvation is sensible.

The reasonableness of the incarnation, and the reasonableness of communication between God and man, turn on this point, that man, as man, is created in the image of God.

The communication which God has made to man is true, but that does not mean it is exhaustive, an important distinction which we must always bear in mind. To know anything exhaustively we should need to be infinite, as God. Even in heaven we shall not be this.

God has communicated to man, not only about the cosmos and history, but also about Himself. And God's attributes so communicated are meaningful to God, the author of the communication, as well as to man, the recipient of the communication. What God has revealed concerning His attributes is not only meaningful below the line of anthropology. The line of anthropology is not a brazen heaven, which cannot be penetrated, over our heads. The God who has spoken is not the unknowable infinite above the line. The God who has created man in His own image communicates true truth about Himself. Therefore, this need not be thought of as only an existential experience or contentless 'religious ideas'. We have true knowledge, for as the Scriptures say so simply and overwhelmingly, when God wrote the Ten Commandments on stone,[2] or when Jesus spoke to Paul on the Damascus road in the Hebrew language,[3] they used a real language subject to grammars and lexicons, a language to be understood.

When we talk to each other there are three theoretical possibilities in our exchange of words. The first is that we fail to communicate at all, probably because our backgrounds are too far apart. The second possibility is the very opposite of this: that when we use terms we all give to them exactly the same meaning, so that we exhaustively understand each other. Neither of these concepts will stand careful analysis.

The weakness of saying that one is not able to communicate at all was shown up in a conversation I once had with an undergraduate at St. Andrews University. Many had said that they found him difficult to talk to, that what he said did not seem to make sense, and they were at a loss to know where to start. I had half an hour to spend with him. After only two minutes of talking in his room, he said, 'Sir, I don't think we are communicating.' I started again. About two minutes later he repeated himself, 'Sir, I don't think we are communicating.' I began to think that the half-hour would be spent in a nonsense session! I looked down and noticed that he had very thoughtfully prepared a lovely tea. There it all was, pot of tea, cups and so on. So I said rather gruffly to him, 'Give me some tea!' He was taken aback, but he passed me a cup, full of tea. Then I said, 'Sir, I think we are communicating.' From then on we had a very effective conversation!

The simple fact is that no one who takes the trouble to study linguistics really believes that just because we bring our own backgrounds to the words, idioms and phrases we use, we cannot communicate. On the other hand we need to be warned: just because we know what *we* mean by a term does not mean that the person to whom we speak understands precisely the same thing. That would be very naïve. In human conversation we have true communication, but it is never exhaustive. This is the third and only realistic possibility in our speaking to one another.

If we transfer the possibility of communication from the realm of human intercourse to that of the Divine-human, then the same principle applies. The biblical presentation indicates that, because man is made in God's image, the problem of God communicating to him is not of an absolutely different order from that of man speaking to man. We are finite, God is infinite, but we can understand truly.

LOVE IS MORE THAN A WORD

This conception of the way in which God communicates gives a world which is different from the one in which modern man is struggling. It means quite simply that man no longer needs to destroy; there is a reason to live, build and love. Man is no longer adrift. We may demonstrate how different the two worlds are by considering the meaning of love. Modern man quite properly considers the conception of love to be overwhelmingly important as he looks at personality. Nevertheless, he faces a very real problem as to the meaning of love. Though modern man tries to hang everything on the word love, it can easily degenerate into something very much less because he really does not understand it. He has no adequate universal for love.

On the other hand, the Christian does have the adequate universal he needs in order to be able to discuss the meaning of love. Among the things we know about the Trinity is that the Trinity was before the creation of everything else and that love existed between the persons of the Trinity before the foundation of the world.[4] This being so, the existence of love as we know it in our make-up does not have an origin in chance, but its origin is from that which has always been.

Above the line of anthropology, God the Father loved God the Son before the creation of the world—this is on a horizontal plane. On the vertical plane God also loves me who am below the line of anthropology. The word and act of love has crossed the line of anthropology downward. Then, also on the vertical plane, I am to love God. The word and act of love has crossed the line of anthropology upward. Finally, I am commanded by God to love my wife, children, neighbours, below the line of anthropology. Here is the word and act of love horizontally below the line of anthropology.

The relationships of love can be shown like this:

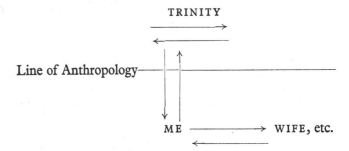

Two things follow from this. Firstly, I can know something truly of what it means when I am told that God the Father loves the Son. When I see a boy and a girl walking together arm in arm, obviously showing love towards each other, I do not know all that they feel towards one another, yet because I too love my woman, my looking at them is not as a dog would look at them. It is not exhaustive, but it is true understanding—there is true correlation. And when I talk about love existing in the Trinity before creation, I am not talking gibberish. Though I am very far from plumbing all its depths when applied to God Himself, yet the word love and the reality of love when Christ spoke of the Father loving Him before the foundation of the world, has true meaning for me.

Secondly, when I love my woman, its meaningfulness is not exhausted by the context of this one individual relationship alone, nor even the love of all men for all women, nor all finite love. The validity and meaning of love rest upon the reality that love exists between the Father and Son in the Trinity. When I say I love, instead of this being a nonsense word, it has meaning. It is rooted in what has always been in the personal relationship existing in the Trinity before the universe was created. Man's love is not a product of chance that has no fulfilment in what has always been. Now, love is a thing not only of meaning but of beauty and wonder to be nourished in joy.

This then is the second great difference between Christianity and the new theology. The latter gives no basis for verifiable facts and knowing, including knowing the content of words used about God above the line of anthropology. Thus, such a word as love has no meaning or value beyond the realm of limited man. *It should be obvious by this time that Christianity and the new theology have no relationship except the use of a common terminology with different meanings.*

CHAPTER 3

The Dilemma of Man

We have considered two areas in which Christianity and the new theology fundamentally disagree—personality and knowledge. There is one more area where disagreement could not be more radical and that is the question of man and his dilemma. Anyone with sensitivity and concern for the world in which he lives can see that man is in a great dilemma. Man is able both to rise to great heights and to sink to great depths of cruelty and tragedy. Modern man is strongly struggling with the concept of man in his dilemma. Most of the paintings of the crucifixion today, for example, Salvador Dali's, are not of Christ dying on the cross in history. They are using the Christ symbol to exhibit Man in agony.

Of course it is possible to try *not* to get involved in man's dilemma; but the only way not to get involved in the dilemma of man is by being young enough, well enough, having money enough, and being egotistic enough to care nothing about other human beings.

As we consider this question of man and his dilemma, only two possible explanations can be given. The first explanation has a *metaphysical cause*. This says, in effect, that man's problem is that he is too small, too finite to wrestle with the factors that confront him. The second explanation is quite different, it puts man's dilemma down to a *moral cause*. If the first explanation is the right one, then one is bound to conclude that man has always been in the same dilemma. Thus, for example, the new theology says that man has always been fallen man. This also means that there is no moral answer to the problem of evil and cruelty. Because man, whether somehow created by a curious thing called god or kicked up out of the slime by chance, has always been in this dilemma, the dilemma is part of what being 'man' is. And if this is what man intrinsically is, and he has always been like this, then the French art historian and poet, Baudelaire, is right when he says, 'If there is a God, he is the devil.' This statement was simply the logical deduction from the premise that man, with all his cruelty and suffering, is now as he always has been. At this point Baudelaire was consistent and refused to give any kind of romantic alternatives as an explanation. But the Bible says that this is not the situation.

One day I was talking to a group of people in the digs of a young South African in Cambridge. Among others, there was present a young Indian who was of Sikh background but a Hindu by religion. He started to speak strongly against Christianity, but did not really understand the problems of his own beliefs. So I said, 'Am I not correct in saying that on the basis of your system, cruelty and non-cruelty are ultimately equal, that there is no intrinsic difference between them?' He agreed. The people who listened and knew him as a delightful person, an 'English gentleman' of the very best kind, looked up in amazement. But the student, in whose room we met, who had clearly understood the implications of what the Sikh had admitted, picked up his kettle of boiling water with which he was about to make tea, and stood with it steaming over the Indian's head. The man looked up and asked him what he was doing and he said, with a cold yet gentle finality, 'There is no difference between cruelty and non-cruelty.' Thereupon the Hindu walked out into the night.

If the metaphysical explanation to man's dilemma is given, it is not an abstraction. In such a case all that moves man at his best is really meaningless.

THE SCANDAL OF THE CROSS

There is a serious commentary given on man and his dilemma in Albert Camus's book *The Plague*.[1] The story is about a plague brought by rats into the city of Oran at the beginning of the Second World War. On the surface it reads like an account of any city that might have been struck by such a tragedy. But Camus intends a deeper understanding. Therefore he confronts the reader with a serious choice: either he must join the doctor and fight the plague, in which case, says Camus, he will then also be fighting God; or he can join with the priest and not fight the plague, and thus be anti-humanitarian. This is the choice; and this is the dilemma which Camus faced and which all those face who, like him, do not have the Christian answer.[2]

However, the new theology has no answer to the dilemma either. Its followers are equally caught in Camus's problem and Baudelaire's proposition. All that is reasonable in their position, based on observing the world as it is, says that God is the devil. Nevertheless, because they cannot live with this conclusion, by an act of blind faith they say God is good. This, they say, is what the 'scandal of the cross' is—to believe that God is good against all the evidence open to reason. But, this is emphatically not the 'scandal of the cross'. The true scandal is that however faithfully and clearly one preaches the Gospel, at a certain point, the world, because it is in rebellion, will turn from it. Men turn away not because what is said makes no sense, but because they do not want to bow before the God who is there. This is the 'scandal of the cross'.

Modern theology may use the *term* guilt, but because it is not orientated in a true moral framework, it turns out to be no more than guilt-feelings. And as in their system they have no place for true guilt, the death of Jesus on the Cross takes on an entirely different meaning. Following from this, the work of Christ and the ministry of the Church becomes one of two things: either a basis for sociological motivation, using undefinable religious terms; or a means for psychological integration, again using religious words. In both cases the connotation words used are open to the controlling of the manipulators.

There is a contrary danger. That is that the orthodox Christian will fail to realise that at times guilt-feelings are present when no true guilt exists. Let us remember that the Fall resulted in division not only between God and man, and man and man, but between man and himself. Hence there are psychological guilt-feelings without true guilt. In such cases we must show genuine compassion. But where there is a real moral guilt before the God who is there, this must never be passed off or explained away, as the new theology does, as psychological.

Another result of the position of the new theology is that there is no personal antithesis at the point of justification. For them there can never be a qualitative difference in one's relationship to God. The Christian view is that when a person casts himself on Jesus Christ as Saviour, at that moment he has passed from death to life, from the Kingdom of Darkness to the Kingdom of God's dear Son.[3] It means to be acquitted from true guilt and no longer be condemned. This is an absolute personal antithesis. If, on the other hand, there is no absolute antithesis between moral and immoral, cruel and non-cruel, then the only difference is a quantitative one.

We may not play with the new theology however much we may think we can turn it to our advantage. This means, for example, that we must beware of co-operation in evangelistic enterprises in which we are forced into a position of accepting the new theology as Christian. If we do this, we have cut the ground from under the biblical concept of the personal antithesis of justification.

Because the new theology has no place for antithesis, and because for its proponents sin and guilt is, in the last analysis, a metaphysical and not a moral problem, they have either an implicit or explicit universalism regarding man's ultimate salvation. It is naïve for evangelicals to regard this universalism as merely an unrelated corner of the neo-orthodox system. It may not always be explicit in the teaching of the new theologians, but we must see that the logic of their views concerning man's dilemma irresistibly drives them to this position. At this point their beliefs hang together very well. They have no final antithesis between right and wrong, therefore there can be no such thing as true moral guilt; therefore justification as a radically changed relationship with God can have no meaning; therefore no one is finally condemned. On the basis of their system this is a perfectly consistent and necessary position to hold and universalism is naturally related to what their system is.

HISTORIC CHRISTIANITY AND MAN'S DILEMMA

The historic Christian position is that man's dilemma has a moral cause. God, being non-determined, created man as a non-determined person. This is a difficult idea to anyone thinking in twentieth-century terms because most twentieth-century thinking sees man as determined. He is determined either by chemical factors, as the Marquis de Sade held and Dr. Francis Crick is trying to prove, or by psychological factors, as Freud and others have suggested. In either case, or as a result of the fusion of these two, man is considered to be programmed. If this is the case, then man is not the tremendous thing the Bible says he is, made in the image of God as a personality who could make a free first choice. Because God created a true universe outside of Himself (not as an extension of His essence), there is a true history which exists. Man as created in God's image is therefore a significant man in a significant history, who could choose to obey the commandment of God and love Him, or revolt against Him. There is no reformed theologian, however strong his reformed theology might be, who would not say that Adam in this way was able fundamentally to change the course of history.

This is the wonder of man and the wonder of history. It is the very opposite of the Zen-Buddhist statement which says, 'The mind of man is like the wind in a pine tree in a Chinese ink drawing.' In this man is killed twice. He is only the wind in the pine tree, and even this is only in a drawing. Christianity teaches the very reverse of what the Eastern thinker says. Man can understand and respond to the One who, having made him and communicated with him, called upon him to show that he loved Him by simple command, 'Don't do this'. The test could have been something else. No act of primitive magic is involved here. This is the infinite-personal God calling on personal man to act by choice. And it was a motivated command, '. . . for in the day that you eat of it you shall surely die',[4] which would make no sense if man is only a machine. He could so act by choice because he was created to be different from the animal, the plant and the machine.

To ask that man should have been made so that he *was not able* to revolt is to ask that God's creation should have ceased after He created plants and animals. It is to ask that man should be reduced to machine programming. It is to ask that man should not exist.

If one begins to consider the Christian system as a total system, one must begin with the infinite-personal triune God who is there, and who was communicating and loving before anything else was. If one begins to consider how sinful man can return to fellowship with God, one must begin with Christ, His person and work. But if one begins to consider the differences between Christianity and rationalistic philosophy's answers, one must begin with understanding that man and history are now abnormal. It is not that philosophy and Christianity deal with absolutely different questions; but that historic Christianity and rationalistic philosophy differ at this point (whether man and history are now normal or abnormal), and they differ in that rationalistic thinking starts with only the knowledge finite man can glean for himself.[5]

Christianity says man is now abnormal—he is separated from his Creator, who is his only sufficient reference point—not by a metaphysical limitation, but by true moral guilt. As a result he is now also separated from his fellow men, from nature and from himself. Therefore, when he is involved in cruelty, he is not being true to what he was initially created to be. Cruelty is a symptom of abnormality and a result of a moral, historic, space-time Fall.

What does a historic space-time Fall involve? It means that there was a period before man fell; that, if you had been there, you could have seen Adam before he fell; that, at the point when he revolted against God by making a free choice to disobey God's commandment, there was a tick of the clock. Take away the first three chapters of Genesis, and you cannot maintain a true Christian position nor give Christianity's answers.

CHAPTER 4

God's Answer to Man's Dilemma

With the Christian answer it is now possible to understand that there are true moral absolutes. There is no Law behind God, because the furthest thing back *is* God. The moral absolutes rest upon God's character. The creation as He originally made it conformed to His character. The moral commands He has given to men are an expression of His character. Men as created in His image are to live by choice on the basis of what God is. The standards of morality are determined by what conforms to His character, while those things which do not conform are immoral.

God can know about things that are not actualised. For example, he knew all about Eve, but she was not actualised until He made her. The same thing can be true in the area of morals. When man sins he brings forth what is contrary to the moral Law of the universe and as a result he is morally and legally guilty. Because man is guilty before the Law-giver of the universe, doing what is contrary to His character, his sin is significant and he is morally significant in a significant history. Man has true moral guilt. This is entirely different from the conception of modern thought, which states that actions do not lead to guilt, which actions thus become morally meaningless. Even the most degraded actions of sin have no moral meaning. Ultimately 'good' and 'bad' actions alike are zero. This is an important factor in modern man seeing Man as zero.

The Christian answer begins by saying that man is a moral creature made in the image of the Creator; that there is a law in the universe which, if broken, means that man is culpable. In this view, man is morally significant both as far as God is concerned and as far as his fellow men are concerned. The modern non-Christian answer denies the legitimacy of moral absolutes, refuses to pass any kind of moral comment on man's actions and thus reduces cruel and non-cruel deeds to the same level. With this answer not only is the concept of sin reduced to less than the biblical concept but *man* is reduced to less than the biblical concept of guilty man.

If the modern explanation is accepted, then there ceases to be an answer to man's dilemma—man is as he was in the beginning and ever will be. With the moral explanation of man's position in the universe and his consequent dilemma following the Fall, there is a possible solution to his problems.

If there is true moral guilt in the presence of a personal God (rather than a metaphysical intrinsic situation of what is and always has been) then perhaps there will be a solution from God's side; and God says to man, there is a solution. I am holy and I am love, and in my love I have loved the world, and I sent my Son. Now in history, there on Calvary's cross, in space and time, Jesus died. Never speak of Jesus' death without linking it to His person. This is the eternal second person of the Trinity. When He died, with the division that man has caused by his revolt now carried up into the Trinity itself, there in expiation, in propitiation and substitution, the true moral guilt is met by the *infinite* value of Jesus' death. Thus Jesus says: 'It is finished.'

Romans 3:26 is a verse that we tend to pass by too quickly in the midst of the structure of the first three chapters of Romans, which chapters tell us first why man is lost, and then the solution in the propitiatory death of Jesus Christ. At this point Paul can say: 'that he himself might be just and *yet* (the force of the Greek construction) the justifier of him who has faith in Jesus'. On the one hand, because of the infinite value of Christ's death, God does not have to surrender His absolutely holy character; and on the other, He does not have to violate man's significance in order for Him to be able to pardon guilt and restore man's broken relationship to Himself. This is the very opposite of the denial of antithesis and significance in modern man's leap into the dark, which says that somehow we must believe without reason that God is love. A moral absolute remains, and yet there is a solution to man's dilemma.

THERE NEED BE NO EITHER—OR IN *La Peste*

From the biblical answer flow four important facts.

Firstly, the God who is there is a good God.

Secondly, there is a hope of a solution to the dilemma of man.

Thirdly, there is a sufficient basis for morals. Nobody has ever discovered a way of having real 'morals', without a moral absolute. If there is no moral absolute we are left with hedonism (doing what *I* like) or some form of the social contract theory (what is best for society as a whole is right). However, neither of these alternatives corresponds to the moral motions that men have, nor to what men mean when they speak of morals. Without absolutes, morals as morals cease to exist, and humanistic man starting from himself has failed to find the absolute. But because the God of the Bible is there, real morals exist. Within this framework I can say one action is right and another wrong, without talking nonsense.

Fourthly, there is an adequate reason for fighting wrong. The Christian never faces the dilemma posed in Camus's book *La Peste*. It simply is not true that he either has to side with the doctor against God by fighting the plague, or join with the priest on God's side and thus be much less than human by not fighting the plague.[1] If this were an *either—or* choice in life it would be truly terrible.[2] But the Christian is not consigned to such a choice. Let us go to the tomb of Lazarus. As Jesus stood there, He not only wept but He was *angry*. The exegesis of the Greek of the passages John 11:33 and 38 is clear.[3] Jesus, standing in front of the tomb of Lazarus, was *angry* at death and at the abnormality of the world; the destruction and distress caused by sin. In Camus's words, Christ hated the plague. The point is that He claimed to be God and *He could hate the plague without hating Himself as God.*

A Christian can fight with compassion what is wrong in the world and know that as he hates these things, God hates them too. God hates them to the high price of the death of Christ.

But if one lives in a world of non-absolutes and would fight social injustice on the mood of the moment, how may one establish what social justice is? What criterion do I have to distinguish between right and wrong so that I may know what I should be fighting? May it not be that I could acquiesce in evil and stamp out good? The word 'love' cannot tell me how I may discern, for within the humanistic framework, love can have no defined meaning. But once we comprehend that the Christ who came to die to end 'the plague' both wept and was angry at the plague's effects, we have a reason for fighting that does not rest merely on my momentary disposition, or the shifting consensus of men.

But the Christian also needs to be challenged at this point. The fact that he alone has a sufficient standard upon which to fight evil, does not mean that he *will* so fight. The Christian is the real radical of our generation, for he stands against the monolithic, modern concept of truth as relative—we believe in the unity of truth. But too often, instead of being the radical, standing against the shifting sands of relativism, he subsides into merely maintaining the *status quo*. If it is true that evil is evil, that God hates it to the point of the cross and that there is a moral law fixed in what God is in Himself, then Christians should be the first into the field against what is wrong—including man's inhumanity to man.

CHAPTER 5

How do We Know It is True?

All men on their own level face a problem. Confronted with the existence and form of the external universe and the 'mannishness' of man, how does it fit together, and what sense does it make?

Imagine a book which has been mutilated, leaving just one inch of printed matter on each page. Although it would obviously be impossible to piece together and understand the book's story, yet few people would imagine that what had been left had come together by chance. However, if the torn off parts of each page were found in the attic and were added in the right places, then the story could be read and would make sense. The whole man would be relieved that the mystery of the book had been solved and the whole man would be involved in the reading of the completed story; but man's reason would have been the first to tell him that the portions which were discovered were the proper solution to the problem of the ripped book.

Notice two things about this illustration. Firstly, the portions of each page left in the book could never tell what the story was about. Their importance was as a test to determine whether the pieces found in the attic were the right ones for that book. Secondly, the man who discovered the matching portions used his reason to show that they fitted the mutilated book but then, on the level of his whole personality, he enjoyed reading and understanding the complete story of the original pieces and the added portions. This would particularly be the case if the *total* book opened the way to a restored communication with someone important to the reader.

So it is with Christianity: the ripped pages remaining in the book correspond to the abnormal universe and the abnormal man we now have. The parts of the pages which are discovered correspond to the Scriptures which are God's propositional communication to mankind, which not only touch 'religious' truth but also touch the cosmos and history which are open to verification. Neither the abnormal external world nor the abnormal 'mannishness' of man can give the answer to the whole meaning of the created order, yet they are both important in knowing that the Scriptures, God's communication to man, are what they claim to be. The question is whether the communication given by God completes and explains the portions we had before and especially whether it explains what was obvious before, though without an explanation—that is, that the universe and the 'mannishness' of man are not just a chance configuration of the printer's scrambled type. To put it in another way, does the Bible's answer or does John Cage's chance music speak of what exists?

Man rationalistically and autonomously could not give a proper answer on the basis of the portion of the book that remained. Without the pages which were discovered, man would never have had the answer. Neither do we have a leap of faith, because the pieces match up in a coherent whole over the whole unified field of knowledge. With the propositional communication from the personal God before us, not only the things of the cosmos and history match up but everything on the upper and lower storeys matches too; grace and nature; a moral absolute and morals; the universal point of reference and the particulars, and the emotional and aesthetic realities of man as well.

Of course, the individual man will not see that they match up if he rejects the communication just because he has not thought it up himself. This would be much the same as rejecting the pieces of a book found in the attic because he wanted to make up his own story.

THE NATURE OF PROOF

In dealing with the question of proof which has been raised by the illustration of the book, I want to suggest that scientific proof, philosophical proof and religious proof follow the same rules. We may have any problem before us which we wish to solve; it may concern a chemical reaction or the meaning of man. After the question has been defined, in each case proof consists of two steps:

A.   The theory must be non-contradictory and must give an answer to the phenomenon in question.

B.   We must be able to live consistently with our theory. For example, the answer given to the chemical reaction must conform to what we observe in the test tube. With regard to man and his 'mannishness', the answer given must conform to what we observe in a wide consideration of man and how he behaves.

Specifically in relation to the question of man, does the Christian answer conform to and explain what we observe concerning man as he is (including my knowledge of myself as a man)? The

Christian answer is that man is not dead, but rather that intrinsically he was man and personal from the time he was made by a personal source; and though at the beginning he was normal, he is now abnormal. The reader may well recall here the illustration of the water rising in the second valley and the material in the previous chapters which dealt with the personal source and with man's present abnormality.

Then there is the negative consideration. After a careful definition has weeded out the trivial, the other possible answers that do not involve a mystical leap of faith are of the following nature:

1. That the impersonal plus time plus chance have produced a personal man. But this theory is against all experience and thus usually the advocates of this theory end with a leap of faith, often hidden by the use of connotation words.

2. That man is not personal, but dead. That he is in reality a machine and therefore personality is an illusion. This theory could fit the first criterion of being non-contradictory, but it will not fit the second, for man simply cannot live as though he were a machine. This may be observed as far back in the history of man as we have evidence—for example, from the art artifacts of the caves or from man's burial rites. We have already given many examples of the way in which a man, such as a scientist in love, has been driven to a Jekyll and Hyde existence on the basis of this conclusion. He is one thing in his laboratory, but someone completely different at home with his wife and children, or on the left bank of the Seine with his arms around his girl. Included is the whole struggle of modern man, the despair shown by the acceptance of the irrational leap in a desperate attempt to have answers at the expense of reason, and the scream of the modern artists when they do not find a meaning for man. Although man may say that he is no more than a machine, his whole life denies it.

3. That in the future man will find another reasonable answer. There are, however, two overwhelming problems to this answer: *firstly*, this could be said about any answer to anything and would bring all thought and science to an end. It must be said to be an evasion of the issue and a very weak reply if the person using it only applies it to this one question. *Secondly*, no one can live with this answer, for it simply is not possible to hold one's breath and wait till some solution is found in the future. All the while the individual must make moral judgments which affect himself and others and he must be using some working hypothesis from which to start. Thus, if a person is to offer this seriously as an alternative theory, he should be prepared to go into deep freeze and stop

making judgments which touch on the problem of man. Bertrand Russell, for example, should stop making sociological decisions which involve others. This position is only possible if one stops the clock.

4. That the scientific theory of relativity may in the future prove to be a sufficient answer for human life. But the scientific theory of relativity cannot be applied to human life in this way. The scientific theory is constantly being tested, both as a theory and by measurement, and therefore it does not mean that 'anything goes', as it does when relativity is applied to human values. Moreover, the speed of light in a vacuum is considered to be an absolute standard. Therefore, scientific relativity does not imply that all scientific laws are in a constant state of flux, as is the case when this idea is applied to man.

One might think of a few other attempts to find possible answers, but the possibilities are very few indeed.

In contrast to such answers, if the scope of the phenomena under consideration is large enough (that is if it includes the existence of the universe and its form,[1] and the 'mannishness' of man as he now is) Christianity, beginning with the existence of the infinite-personal God, man's creation in His image and a space-time Fall, constitutes a non-self-contradictory answer that does explain the phenomena and which can be lived with, both in life and in scholarly pursuits.

I would suggest that a serious question would have to be faced as to whether the reason why modern men reject the Christian answer, or why they often do not even consider it, is *because they have already accepted with an implicit faith the presupposition of the uniformity of natural causes in a closed system.*

This does not mean that the Christian answer should be accepted for pragmatic reasons, but it does mean that the solution given in the Bible answers the problem of the universe and man and nothing else does.

It should be added in conclusion that the Christian, after he is a Christian, has years of experimental evidence to add to all the above reasons, but we may stop at the same place as Paul in Romans 1, by saying that the existence of the external universe and its form and the 'mannishness' of man demonstrate the truth of the historic Christian position. He does not in Romans 1 go on to appeal to the Christian's experience. 'For the wrath of God is revealed from heaven against all ungodliness and unrighteousness of men, who hold down the truth in unrighteousness; because that which may be known of God is manifest in them [the 'mannishness' of man], for God manifested it unto them. For the invisible things of him since the creation of the world are clearly seen, being perceived through the things that are made [the external world and its form], even his everlasting power and divinity, that they may be without excuse.'[2]

TRUE RATIONALITY BUT NOT ONLY RATIONALITY

Although rationality is important, it should never become exclusively so.[3] Rationality is not the end of the matter. It is parallel to the problem of form and freedom in art. The artist, to be an artist, needs to be free. On the other hand, if there is no form to his painting, the artist loses all communication with the viewers. The form makes it possible for the artist to have freedom plus communication. In the same way rationality is needed to open the door to a vital relationship to God.

The study of verbalised and non-verbalised communication enters here. What form is to the artist, words are in general communication. The use of words clearly defined and dealt with rationally gives form and certainty in communication. The same thing is true with carefully defined scientific symbols.

It is possible to add things to the verbalisation, dealt with rationally, and thus enrich it. For example, poetry undoubtedly adds something to prose form. In the Psalms something is communicated to us which would not be so in a bare prose account. The same thing is true when the artist paints a portrait. However, if there is an absolute divorce between the defined verbalisation rationally comprehended on the one hand and (for example) *bare poetic form* on the other, no certain communication comes across to the reader. The most the reader can do is to use the bare poetic form as a quarry out of which his own emotions can create something.

As long as a genuine continuity remains between the defined verbalisation and what is added, then all kinds of enrichment can be brought in. But if there is discontinuity, then there is no one who can say for certain what the added things mean. This is true in art, in experience and even in using a figure of speech. Figures of speech enhance communication so long as they fit into a framework of defined speech which can be rationally considered. But if someone wrote a book or a play which was composed only of figures of speech without any relation to a defined rational context, not only would communication be lost, but the purpose of the figure of speech itself (to be enriching) would be lost.

Therefore it is not that rationality is exclusively important, but rather that rationality defines and provides a form for the whole.

In the Scriptures there is a good example of this when John lays down as the only true test of the spirits and prophets something which has content and is rationally based: 'Beloved, believe not every spirit, but prove the spirits, whether they are of God: because many false prophets are gone out into the world. Hereby know ye the Spirit of God: every spirit which confesseth that Jesus Christ is come in the flesh is of God: and every spirit that confesseth not Jesus is not of God: and this is the spirit of the antichrist.'[4]

The Christian is not rationalistic, he does not try to begin from himself autonomously and work out a system from there on. But he is rational: he thinks and acts on the basis that A is not non-A. However, he does not end with only rationality, for in his response to what God has said his whole personality is involved. Yet, if the control of defined verbalisation is lost, then we lose our way. There is no longer any means of testing the spirits, the prophets or experience. All of this then becomes merely the Greek shade in the upper storey of the new theology about which we spoke earlier.

It is therefore most important to get the balance between the truly rational on the one hand, and the involvement of the whole man at every level on the other, as something which flows on from the first. Much can be added to the rational, but if we give up the rational everything will be lost.

It will help us to clarify this if we go back to the illustration of the ripped book. It is the reason which is involved in knowing that the communication is the truth of what is; but then, it is the whole man who rejoices in the finding of the missing answer and in the reading of the now *combined* pieces. These combined pieces give knowledge of the infinite-personal God who is there and show how communication with Him may be restored. Reason began the process, and from then on the whole man is involved.

Recently I was at a discussion group in Detroit. An older Negro pastor was there. We discussed many intellectual and cultural problems and the answers given by Christianity. One would have called the discussion intellectual rather than devotional. As he was leaving the Negro pastor shook my hand and thanked me. If he had said, 'Thank you for helping me to defend my people better', or 'Thank you for helping me to be a better evangelist', I would have been very glad that what I had said had been helpful, and then possibly I would not have given it another thought. But what he actually said was, 'Thank you for opening these doors for me; now I can worship God better'. I will never forget him because he was a man who really understood. If this is not our response first of all, and then the response of those whom we try to help, we have made a mistake somewhere.

WHO STANDS IN THE CONTINUITY OF THE CHURCH?

We have now discussed very many radical differences between historic Christianity and the new theology, which is the fifth step in the line of despair. A question may arise here. In the light of the nature of the new theology, how is it that these modern theologians claim to stand in the continuity of the Church?

I think the key to their claim is that they have changed the meaning of continuity. According to them, the continuity of the Church has nothing to do with content.

As far as historic Christianity is concerned, continuity in the Church is maintained by a well-defined content. The Old Testament teaches a certain content, the New Testament amplifies this so that, though one is fuller than the other, the content is the same. Further on in the history of the Church we find the great Creeds, a classification of the same content, as given in the Scriptures. Right through the teaching of the reformers and men like Samuel Rutherford, Charles Hodge and down to the present day, we find the same content. Therefore, if I, as an individual, look at the content of what I hold to as Christianity and it is the same as this, then I can know that I am in the continuity of the Church as well. Continuity rests upon a content which can be known.

In contrast, the new theology has little or no place for content. For its proponents, the continuity of the Church rests and turns on the *experience* which men have had down the ages. The men of the Old Testament, the men of the Early Church, the men of the Creeds and the Reformation and so on, all had experiences. It is not that the content of the experiences is the same, nor even that there is any content. It is the existence of experience as such which gives the continuity.

We emphasised earlier that one of the great problems in discussing existential experiences is that they cannot be communicated. One can neither communicate them to one another, nor to oneself. How then do the new theologians view the Bible? They would say this: surrounding each of the men who wrote what makes up the Bible there was a cultural pattern. This pattern was full of mistakes, mistakes of a primitive age and of man because he is finite, and they correspond to the writer's own level of cultural advancement. Therefore what the writers said was intrinsically linked up with the mistakes of the culture in which they happened to live. They expressed themselves in the faulty thought-forms of the day. When they had an existential experience, this too was expressed verbally in a way which reflected the errors in thinking of their contemporary surroundings.

Consequently, as the reader goes back to the Bible he must realise that what he reads is *inevitably* full of mistakes, because of the era in which it was written. *The words of the text are already an interpretation of experiences, the content of which cannot be known.*

This is their view and what matters in maintaining the Church's continuity, so far as the new theology is concerned, is that there *was* an experience and there *is* an experience, and an illusion of communication concerning these experiences is carried on by the use of the religious connotation words.

Speaking Historic Christianity into the Twentieth-Century Climate

CHAPTER I

Finding the Point of Tension

COMMUNICATING TO ONE OF MY KIND

Communication means that an idea which I have in my mind passes through my lips (or fingers—in most art forms) and reaches the other person's mind. Adequate communication means that when it reaches the recipient's mind it is substantially the same as when it left mine. This does not mean that it will be completely the same, but that he will nevertheless have substantially realised the point I wish to convey. The words that we use are only a tool for translating the ideas which we wish to communicate; we are not trying to convey merely a succession of verbal sounds.

Because we must use words in order to communicate ideas, there may be several language problems. The most obvious arises where the differences between different language groups are concerned. If we want to speak to a man, we must learn his language first.

Another difference is that of time. In the course of history language changes in meaning, so that the same words may not have the same meaning today as they did in an earlier age. Language naturally changes its meaning as time passes, and this is uniquely true today with the great differences above and below the line of despair.

A further language barrier comes as we try to talk to people of a very different social background from ourselves, for example those in the deep slums.

In none of these cases do the language problems solve themselves automatically. If we wish to communicate, then we must take time and trouble to learn our hearers' use of language so that they understand what we intend to convey. This is particularly difficult today for a Christian, who wants to use a word like 'God' or 'guilt' in a strictly defined sense rather than as a connotation word, because the concepts of these words have universally been changed. In a case like this, either we must try to find a synonymous word without a false connotation, or else we have to define the word at length when we use it, so that we make sure our hearer understands as fully as possible what we are conveying. In this latter case we are no longer using the word as a technical word in the sense that we assume a common definition.

I would suggest that if the word (or phrase) we are in the habit of using is no more than an orthodox evangelical cliché which has become a technical term among Christians, then we should be willing to give it up when we step outside our own narrow circle and talk to the men about us. If, on the other hand, the word is indispensable, such as the word 'God', then we should talk at sufficient length to make ourselves clear. Technical words, if they are used without sufficient explanation, may mean that outsiders really do not hear the Christian message at all and that we ourselves, in our churches and missions, have become an introverted and isolated language group.

As we turn to consider in more detail how we may speak to men of the twentieth century, we must emphasise first of all that we cannot apply mechanical rules. We, of all people, should realise this, for as Christians we believe that personality really does exist and is important. We can lay down some general principles but there can be no automatic application. If we are truly personal, as created by God, then each individual will differ from everyone else. Therefore each man must be dealt with as an individual, not as a case or statistic or machine. If we would work with these people, we cannot mechanically apply the things of which we have been speaking in this book. We must look to the Lord in prayer, and to the work of the Holy Spirit, for effective use of these things.

Furthermore, we must remember that the person to whom we are talking, however far from the Christian faith he may be, is an image-bearer of God. He has great value and our communication to him must be in genuine love. Love is not an easy thing; it is not just an emotional urge, but an attempt to move over and sit in the other person's place and see how his problems look to him. Love is a genuine concern for the individual. As Jesus Christ reminds us, we are to love him 'as ourselves'. This is the place to begin. Therefore, to be engaged in personal 'witness' as a duty or because our Christian circle exerts a social pressure on us, is to miss the whole point. The reason we do it is that this one before us is the image-bearer of God, and he is an individual who is unique in the world. This kind of communication is not cheap. To understand and speak to sincere but utterly confused twentieth-century people is costly. It is tiring; it will open you to temptations and pressures. Genuine love, in the last analysis, means a willingness to be entirely exposed to the person to whom we are talking.

The one before us is our kind. The Bible teaches that there are two humanities, yet, looking at it another way, there is only one humanity. There are two humanities in the sense that there are those still in rebellion against God and there are those who have returned to God through Jesus Christ. But this should not dull us to the fact that God 'hath made of one blood all nations of men for to dwell on all the face of the earth'.[1] This does not just mean that the whole human race is biologically one, in the sense that we can reproduce together, but that we are all descended from Adam as a common ancestor. Thus, emotionally as well as intellectually, we must look at the man before us as *our kind*. This man is our counterpart; he is lost, but so once were we. We are one flesh, one blood, one kind.

Finally, as we consider how we are to communicate to man, we must bear in mind that we are speaking to him as a unit. I am not merely dealing with just one part of him called 'soul' in an attempt to get that to heaven. Rather, I am conscious that the Bible teaches the unity of the personality and, as I try to communicate in this wholeness, this must be reflected in my attitude, as well as in what I say.

LOGICAL CONCLUSIONS

We can look now at some of the general principles to guide our communication with twentieth-century man.

Let us remember that every person we speak to, whether shop girl or university student, has a set of presuppositions, whether they have analysed them or not. The dot in the diagram represents the person's non-Christian presuppositions; the arrow points to what would be the logical conclusion of those non-Christian presuppositions.

A man with his non-Christian presuppositions	●———————→	The logical conclusion of his non-Christian presuppositions

If a man were completely logical to his own presuppositions, he would come out at the line on the right. If he arrived there in thinking and life, he would be consistent to his presuppositions.

But, in fact, no non-Christian can be consistent to the logic of his presuppositions. The reason for this is simply that a man must live in reality, and reality consists of two parts: the external world and its form, and man's 'mannishness', including his own 'mannishness'. No matter what a man may believe, he cannot change the reality of what is. As Christianity is the truth of what is there, to deny this, on the basis of another system, is to stray from the real world:

The real world— the external world and man himself	←————————→	The logical conclusion of a man's non-Christian presuppositions

Every man, therefore, irrespective of his system, is caught. As he tries intellectually to extend his position in a logical way and then live within it, he is caught by the two things which, as it were, slap him across the face. Without indicating that his psychology or philosophy is correct, Carl Gustav Jung has correctly observed that two things cut across every man's will—the external world with its structure, and those things which well up from inside himself. Non-Christian presuppositions simply do not fit into what God has made, including what man is.

This being so, every man is in a place of tension. Man cannot make his own universe and then live in it. Thus, Picasso was not able to make his own world, even on his canvas, and be in the position of God, and, at the same time, communicate to the people looking at his painting. But the problem is deeper even than this, for if he pursued his position logically to its conclusion, he could not consistently communicate even with himself. It would separate him not only from the real world, but from the real self that he is.

The Bible takes this point a step further when it says that, even in hell, a man cannot be consistent to his non-Christian presuppositions; 'If I make my bed in hell, behold, thou (God) art there.'[2] Man will be separated from communion with God in hell, but no one is going to be able to form hell to make their own universe in a limited area. Man, there, will still be in the universe of God. Hence, even in hell, a man cannot be consistent to his non-Christian presuppositions.

In this present life it is the same. It is impossible for any non-Christian individual or group to be consistent to their system in logic or in practice. Thus, when you face twentieth-century man, whether he is brilliant or an ordinary man of the street, a man of the university or the docks, you are facing a man in tension; and it is this tension which works on your behalf as you speak to him. If I did not know this from the Word of God and personal experience, I would not have the courage to step into the circles I do. A man may try to bury the tension and you may have to help him find it, but somewhere there is a point of inconsistency. He stands in a position which he cannot pursue to the end; and this is not just an intellectual concept of tension, it is what is wrapped up in what he is as a man.

Christian apologetics do not start somewhere beyond the stars. They begin with man and what he knows about himself. When a man is lost, he is lost against all that there is, including what he is. Therefore, when he stands before God in judgment, God, in order to point out how false his position has been, will only need to refer to what that man has known of the external world and 'mannish-ness'. As far as morals are concerned, man will only have to be judged according to the standards he himself has laid down in condemning others, for, as Paul makes clear, he then proceeds deliberately to break even his own standards.[3]

Hence, the person before you is not in a vacuum. He knows something of the external world, and he knows something of himself.

Every man is somewhere along the line between the real world and the logical conclusion of his non-Christian presuppositions. Every person feels the pull of two consistencies, the pull towards the real world and the pull towards the logic of his system. He may let the pendulum swing back and forth between them, but he cannot live in both places at once. He will be living nearer to the one or to the other, depending on the strength of the pull at any given time. To have to choose between one consistency or the other is a real damnation for man. *The more logical a man is to his own presuppositions, the further he is from the real world; and the nearer he is to the real world, the more illogical he is to his presuppositions.*

THE TENSIONS ARE FELT IN DIFFERING STRENGTHS

We have said that every person, however intelligent or lacking in intelligence, has stopped somewhere along the line towards the consistent conclusion of his own position. Some people are pre-pared to go further than others, away from the real world, in order to be more logical to their presuppositions. The French existen-tialists Camus and Sartre, exhibit this:

The real world— the external world and man himself	Camus Sartre ←—|————|—→	The logical conclusion of a man's non-Christian presuppositions

Sartre said that Camus was not sufficiently consistent on the basis of their mutual presuppositions. The reason he did this was because Camus never gave up hope, centred in random personal happiness, against the logic of his position. Or again because, as was stated when Camus received the Nobel prize, he never gave up the search for morals, though the world seemed to be without meaning. These are the reasons why, of the two, Camus was more loved in the intellectual world. He never got the real world sorted out, as we have seen from his book *The Plague*, but he was nearer to it than Sartre.

Sartre was correct to say that Camus was illogical to their presuppositions; but, as we saw before, he could not be consistent either. When he signed the Algerian Manifesto, taking a position as though morals have real meaning, he too was being inconsistent to his presuppositions. Thus Sartre is also in tension.

Each person may move up or down the line at different times in their lives, according to their circumstances, but most people more or less stabilise at one point. Every non-Christian, whether he is sleeping under the bridges in Paris or is totally bourgeois, is somewhere along the line.

| The real world—
the external world
and man himself | ←———————|———————→ | The logical conclusion
of a man's non-Christian
presuppositions |

This is not an abstraction, for each of these persons is created in the image of God, and thus is in tension because, within himself, there are things which speak of the real world. Men in different cultures have different standards of morals, but there are no men who do not have some moral motions. Follow a modern girl through her day in London. She may seem totally amoral. But if you were to get to know her you would find that, at some point, she felt the pull of morals. Love may carry different expressions, but all men have some motions of love. The individual will feel this tension in different ways—with some it will be beauty, with some it will be significance, with some it will be rationality, with some it will be the fear of non-being.

Man today seeks to deflect this tension by saying that he is no more than a machine. If he were no more than a machine he would find no difficulty in proceeding step by step down the line to the logical conclusion of his non-Christian presuppositions. But man is not a machine, even if he says he is.

Supposing that a satellite were put into orbit around the earth with a camera that was able to photograph everything on the world's surface. If this information was then fed back to a giant computer that did not need programming, it might calculate that everything behaved mechanically. But the final observer is not a computer but the individual man. There is always one person in the room who does not allow me to see everything as machine-like—it is myself, the observer, because I know myself.

Christians must be careful at this place. Because the Bible says men are lost, it does not say they are nothing. When a man says he is a machine or nothing, he makes himself less than the Bible's view of fallen man.

Therefore, the first consideration in our apologetics for modern man, whether factory-hand or research student, is to find the place where his tension exists. We will not always find it easy to do this. Many people have never analysed their own point of tension. Since the Fall man is separated from himself. Man is complicated and he tries to bury himself in himself. Therefore, it will take time and it will cost something to discover what the person we are speaking to often has not yet discovered for himself. Down inside of himself man finds it easy to lie to himself. We, in love, looking to the work of the Holy Spirit, must reach down into that person and try to find where the point of tension is.

CHAPTER 2

From the Point of Tension to the Gospel

WHY THERE IS A PLACE FOR CONVERSATION[1]

If the man before you were logical to his non-Christian presuppositions you would have no point of communication with him. It would be impossible to have communication if he were consistent. But in reality no one can live logically according to his own non-Christian presuppositions, and consequently, because he is faced with the real world and himself, in *practice* you will find a place where you can talk. He would not be where he is, suspended between the real world and the logical conclusions of his presuppositions, if he were consistent. The only reason he can be at the point of tension, nearer to the real world than his presuppositions would logically indicate, is because, to some extent, he is not logical; and the nearer he is to the real world, the more illogical he is to his presuppositions. As an illustration: it is illogical for John Cage to pick mushrooms as he does, in a universe which, he says, is intrinsically chance, but, illogically, he does pick them; and thus, you could start talking to him concerning the inadequacy of his system, with its chance music, in relationship to his mushrooms.

In *practice* then, we do have a point for conversation, but this point is not properly to be spoken of as 'neutral'. It exists because, regardless of a man's system, he has to live in God's world. If he were consistent to his non-Christian presuppositions he would be separated from the real universe and the real man, and conversation and communication would not be possible.[2]

In this way it does not seem to me that presuppositional apologetics should be seen as ending conversation with the men about us. On the other hand, to try to work below the line of despair without a clear and defined concept of presuppositional apologetics is simply to destroy the possibility of helping twentieth-century people. There is no use talking today until the presuppositions are taken into account, and especially the crucial presuppositions concerning the nature of truth and the method of attaining truth.

When we have discovered, as well as we can, a person's point of tension, the next step is to push him towards the logical conclusion of his presuppositions:

The real world— ⟶ The logical conclusion
the external world ⟵————|———⟶ of a man's non-Christian
and man himself presuppositions

We ought not first to try to move a man away from what he should deduce from his position but towards it, in the direction of the arrow. We try to move him in the natural direction in which his presuppositions would take him. We are then pushing him towards the place where he ought to be, had he not stopped short.

As I seek to do this I need to remind myself constantly that this is not a game I am playing. If I begin to enjoy it as a kind of intellectual exercise, then I am cruel and can expect no real spiritual results. As I push the man off his false balance, he must be able to feel that I care for him. Otherwise I will only end up by destroying him, and the cruelty and ugliness of it all will destroy me as well. Merely to be abstract and cold is to show that I do not really believe this man to be created in God's image and therefore one of my kind. Pushing him towards the logic of his presuppositions is going to cause him pain; therefore I must not push any further than I need to.

If we find the man ready to receive Christ as Saviour, then by all means let us not talk about presuppositions but tell him the glorious good news. The whole purpose of our speaking to twentieth-century people in this way is not to make them admit that we are right in some personally superior way, nor to push their noses in the dirt, but to make them see their need so that they will listen to the Gospel. As soon as the man before us is ready to listen to the Gospel we do not push him any further, because it is horrible to be propelled in the direction of meaninglessness against the testimony of the external world and the testimony of oneself.

As we get ready to tell him God's answer to his need, we must make sure that he understands that we are talking to him about real *truth*, and not about something vaguely religious which seems to work psychologically. We must make sure that he understands that we are talking about *real guilt* before God and that we are not offering him merely relief for his guilt feelings. We must make sure that he understands that we are talking to him about *history*, and that the death of Jesus was not just an ideal or a symbol but a fact of space and time. If we are talking to a man who would not understand the term 'space-time history' we can say to him, 'Do you believe that Jesus died in the sense that, if you had been there that day, you could have rubbed your finger on the cross and got a splinter in it?' *Until he understands the importance of these three things, he is not ready to become a Christian.*

Push him towards the logic of his position in the area of his own real interests. If he is interested in science, we will push him to the logical conclusion of his position in science. If it is art, then gently and yet firmly we push him from the point of tension to the end of his presuppositions. We must, at all points in the conversation, allow him to ask any question he wants. We cannot say, on the one hand, that we believe in the unity of truth and then, on the other hand, suddenly withdraw from the discussion and tell him to believe on blind authority. He has a right to ask questions. It is perfectly true that not every Christian will proceed in this way, and yet people are brought to Christ by them. For every person who is saved we should be very thankful. But to withdraw by saying or implying 'Keep quiet and just believe' may later lead to spiritual weakness, even if he does become a Christian, for it will leave crucial questions unanswered. Therefore, in the midst of our attempts to press our case, we must be ready to receive blows as well. The more he is a true twentieth-century man the more important it is, if you wish to see him become a Christian, that you should accept the blows of the questions in the name of Jesus Christ, and in the name of truth. On the other hand, keep pressing him back, for *he* must keep answering questions, too. As we take time to study both the modern world in which we live and, more particularly, our Bible, we shall come to know more and more answers. We must have faced the question, 'Is Christianity true?' for ourselves. We must be men of the Scriptures, so that we can know what the content of the biblical system is. Every day of our lives we should be studying the Scriptures to make sure that what we are presenting really is the Christian position, and that we are presenting it as well as possible in our day.

TAKING THE ROOF OFF

Let us think of it in a slightly different way. Every man has built a roof over his head to shield himself at the point of tension:

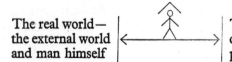

| The real world— the external world and man himself | ←————————→ | The logical conclusion of a man's non-Christian presuppositions |

At the point of tension the person is not in a place of consistency in his system and the roof is built *as a protection against the blows of the real world,* both internal and external. It is like the great shelters built upon some mountain passes to protect vehicles from the avalanches of rock and stone which periodically tumble down the mountain. The avalanche, in the case of the non-Christian, is the real and the abnormal fallen world which surrounds him. The Christian, lovingly and with true tears, must remove the shelter and allow the truth of the external world and of what man is to beat upon him. When the roof is off, each man must stand naked and wounded before the truth of what is.

The truth that we let in first is not a dogmatic statement of the truth of the Scriptures but the truth of the external world and the truth of what man himself is. This is what shows him his need. The Scriptures then show him the nature of his lostness and the answer to it. *This, I am convinced, is the true order for our apologetics in the second half of the twentieth century for man living under the line of despair.*

| The real world— the external world and man himself | | The logical conclusion of a man's non-Christian presuppositions |

It is unpleasant to be submerged by an avalanche, but we must allow the person to undergo this experience in order that he may realise that his system has no answer to the crucial questions of life. He must come to know that his roof is a false protection from the storm of what is, and then we can talk to him of the storm of the Judgment of God.

Removing the roof is not some kind of optional exercise. It is strictly biblical in its emphasis. In the thinking of the twentieth-century man the concept of judgment and of hell is nonsense, and therefore to begin to talk here is to mumble in a language which has no contact with him. Hell or any such concept is unthinkable to modern man because he has been brain-washed into accepting the monolithic belief of naturalism which surrounds him. We of the West are not brain-washed by our State but we are brain-washed by our culture. Even the modern radicals are radicals in a very limited circle.

Before men passed below the line of despair they knew for the most part that they were guilty, but it rarely entered their minds that they were dead as well. On the other hand modern man hardly ever considers himself to be guilty but he often acknowledges that he is dead. The Bible says that both these things are true. Man in revolt against the holy God who is there is guilty and is already under God's wrath. Because he is guilty, he is separated from his true and only reference point and therefore he is dead as well. The Bible does not say man will become lost, but that he is lost. The chasm in biblical teaching does not come at death but at the point of conversion, when the individual passes from death to life. This is the point of personal antithesis, and, before that, man is dead indeed.

Hence we begin to deal with modern man by preaching at the place where he can understand. Often he understands the horrible point of meaninglessness. Often he recognises the tension between the real world and the logic of his presuppositions. Often he appreciates the horror of being dead and yet still alive. The Word of God is overwhelmingly clear in its teaching that there are two aspects of lostness, present and future. When I accept Christ as Saviour, I pass from death to life, *and therefore, before that time I am clearly dead.* Therefore, when modern man feels dead, he is experiencing what the Word of God tells him he is. In himself he will not be able to define his deadness for he does not know what his deadness is, and even less does he know the solution to it, but he is aware of one thing and that is that he is dead. It is our task to tell him that the present death he knows is moral death and not just metaphysical lostness, and then to tell him God's solution. But we begin with the present lostness with which he wrestles. This is not adding to the Gospel, it is applying in practice the depths of the truth of the Word of God, that man in revolt *is* purposeless and dead.

This is what we mean by taking the roof off. But we cannot ever think this to be easy. The hardest thing of all is that when we have exposed modern man to his tension, he still may not be willing for the true solution. Consequently we may seem to leave him in a worse state than he was in before. But this is the same as the evangelism of the past. Whenever the evangelist preached the reality of hell, men who did not believe were more miserable after hearing his preaching than if they had never heard him. We are in the same position. We confront men with reality; we remove their protection and their escapes; we allow the avalanches to fall and, if they then do not become Christians, indeed they are in a worse state than before we spoke to them.

CHAPTER 3

Applying the Gospel

HOW DARE WE DO IT?

How dare we deal with men in this way? Only for one reason—
because Christianity is truth. If we are *not* functioning in the area
that this is absolute truth, such evangelism is cruel beyond
measure. But if this is truth, if it is true that this man before me
is separated from God and lost now and for eternity, then even
though in individual cases men do not accept Christ and are left
worse off than when you began, you must nevertheless have the
courage so to speak. If there is an antithesis, there is an antithesis.
If there is that which is true truth, there is that which is error. If
there is true Christian salvation (in contrast to the concept of
salvation in the new theology), there is lostness.

When I began to approach individuals in this way, some years
ago now, my wife said to me, 'Are you not afraid that someone will
commit suicide one day?' Since then we have had one girl who
tried to do this; fortunately she did not die and later on she made
a profession of faith. But even if she had succeeded, after walking
in the mountains and crying before God, I would begin the same
way with the next person who came.

We cannot do this until we have personally faced the question
as to whether the Judaistic–Christian system is true in the way we
have been speaking of truth. When we are certain about this for
ourselves, then if we love men, we shall have the courage to lift
the roof off other people's lives and expose them to the collapse of
their defences. We ourselves, as we face these people, must have
the integrity to continue to live open to the questions: Does God
exist? Is the content of the Judaistic–Christian system truth?

The more comprehending we are as we take the roof off, the
worse the man will feel if he rejects the Christian answer. In a
fallen world, we must be willing to face the fact that, however
lovingly we preach the Gospel, if a man rejects it, he will be
miserable. It is dark out there. I think that one reason why I am
able to talk to this kind of twentieth-century person is because I
understand something of just how dark it can be. Men must know

that with integrity we have faced the reality of the dark path they are treading.

Once at Cambridge University a post-graduate student said to me, in front of a group that had gathered in his room, 'Mr. Schaeffer, I heard you speak last year. Since then I have been preparing a paper and I would ask you if you would let me read it to you. I dare read it to you because I think you understand. Sir, I am in horror of great darkness.' There is no romanticism as one seeks to move a man in the direction of honesty. On the basis of his system you are pushing him further and further towards that which is not only totally against God, but also against himself. You are pushing him out of the real universe, and of course it hurts, of course it is dark in the place where a man, in order to be consistent to his non-Christian presuppositions, must deny what is there in this life as well as in the next.

Often it is necessary to take much more time to press him towards the logical conclusion of his position than it will later take to give him the answer. Luther spoke of the Law and the Gospel; and the Law, the need, must always be adequately clear first. Then one can give him the Christian answer because he knows his need for something; and one can tell him what his deadness really is, and the solution in the total structure of truth. But if we do not take sufficient time to take the roof off, the twentieth-century man will not comprehend what we are trying to communicate, either as to what his death is caused by, or the solution. We must never forget that the first part of the Gospel is not 'Accept Christ as Saviour', but 'God is there'. Only then are we ready to hear God's solution for man's *moral* dilemma in the substitutionary work of Christ in history.

When we have reached this point with a man, we discover that however complicated modern man may be under the line of despair, however sophisticated or cultured or filled with knowledge, when he sees his need the good news is the same as it has always been. The wonderful thing is that at this point not only can the same ideas be given but even the same words used to all men.

I can recall a time a few years ago when two people professed belief in Christ on the same day. One was a very intelligent doctor, the other a very simple Swiss peasant. In my previous conversations with them, the peasant would have understood little of my talks with the doctor, yet on this day when both of them had come to understand their need, as I spoke first to one and then to the other, I was able to use not only the same ideas, but exactly the same words in telling each one the answer to the need. There is no point in being complicated once the intelligent or the simple man understands his need; the same ideas and even tne same words are all that is now needed.

The problem which confronts us as we approach modern man today is *not* how we are to change Christian teaching in order to make it more palatable, for to do that would mean throwing away any chance of giving the real answer to man in despair; rather it is only a problem of how we may communicate the Gospel so that it is understood.

FAITH IN THE BIBLICAL SENSE

In the first place, Christian faith turns on the reality of God's existence, His being there.[1] Then it also turns on an acceptance of the fact that man's dilemma is moral and not metaphysical. Each person must face these two things on his own level as a matter of truth.

When the Philippian jailer asked Paul and Silas, 'What must I do to be saved?' the passage which follows is: 'Believe on the Lord Jesus, and thou shalt be saved, thou and thy house. And they spake the word of the Lord unto him, with all that were in his house.'[2]

What Paul and Silas said in reply to the question was not spoken in a vacuum. Because of the earthquake and the remarkable way Paul and Silas behaved in prison, the jailer had reason to be aware of the existence of a personal God—one who acts in history, answers prayers and gives men reality in their lives. But this was not all. The whole city had been in an uproar because of all that Paul and Silas had been saying and doing *before* they were put into prison. Finally it would seem, from the preciseness of the jailer's question and from what we know elsewhere of Paul's constant custom, that the jailer had heard the Christian message from Paul himself.

After he had taken them to his house, we read that Paul and Silas spoke to him and his household further of the things of the Lord. Only after this, which we have no reason to think was merely a few minutes' conversation, did they all believe.

True Christian faith rests on content. It is not a vague thing which takes the place of real understanding, nor is it the strength of belief which is of value. *The true basis for faith is not the faith itself, but the work which Christ finished on the cross.* My believing is not the basis for being saved—the basis is the work of Christ. Christian faith is turned outward to an objective person: 'Believe on the Lord Jesus, and thou shalt be saved.'

Once the truth of God's existence is known to us, and we know

133

that we have true moral guilt before a holy God, then we should be glad to know the solution to our dilemma. The solution is from God's side, not ours.

Now the content of God's propositional promises begins to be wonderful to us. Paul and Silas made such a propositional promise to the jailer, and in the Bible God gives such propositional promises more generally. For example, John 3:36 reads: 'He that believeth on the Son hath everlasting life: and he that believeth not the Son shall not see life, but the wrath of God abideth on him.' There is a strong antithesis here. The second part of the verse speaks of man's present and future lostness, the first part of the verse gives God's solution. The call to Christian believing rests on God's propositional promises. We are to consider whether these things are true, but then we are faced with a choice—either we believe Him, or we call God a liar and walk away, unwilling to bow to Him.

As a man is faced with God's promises, Christian faith means bowing twice: *Firstly*, he needs to bow in the realm of Being (metaphysically), that is to acknowledge that he is a creature before the infinite-personal Creator who is there. *Secondly*, he needs to bow in the realm of morals—that is, to acknowledge that he has sinned and therefore that he has true moral guilt before the God who is there. If he has true moral guilt before an infinite God, he has the problem that he, as finite, has no way to remove such a guilt. Thus what he needs is a non-humanist solution. Now he is faced with God's propositional promise, 'Believe on the Lord Jesus, and thou shalt be saved.'

What remains is the meaning of 'believe on the Lord Jesus'. What does it mean to believe on, to cast oneself on, Christ? I would suggest there are four crucial aspects to be considered. More detail could be considered, but these are crucial. They are not slogans to be repeated by rote and they do not have to be said in these words, but the individual must have come to a positive conclusion and affirmation concerning them, if he is to believe in the biblical sense:

1. Do you believe that God exists and that he is a personal God, and that Jesus Christ is God—remembering that we are not talking of the *word* or *idea* god, but of the infinite-personal God who is there?
2. Do you acknowledge that you are guilty in the presence of this God—remembering that we are not talking about guilt-feelings, but true moral guilt?
3. Do you believe that Jesus Christ died in space and time in history on the cross, and that when He died His substitutional

work of bearing God's punishment against sin was fully accomplished and complete?

4. On the basis of God's promises in His written communication to us, the Bible, do you (or have you) cast yourself on this Christ as your personal Saviour—not trusting in anything you yourself have ever done or ever will do?

But note with care that God's promise: 'He that believes on the Son has everlasting life', rests upon: God's being there; Christ being the second person of the Trinity whose death therefore has infinite value; my not coming presumptuously in thinking I can save myself, but casting myself on the finished work of Christ and the written promises of God. My faith is simply the empty hands by which I accept God's free gift.

John Bunyan in *Pilgrim's Progress* has Hopeful say it in this way: 'He [Faithful] bid me go to him and see. Then I said it was presumption. He said, no, for I was invited to come.[3] Then he gave me a book of Jesus' inditing, to encourage me the more freely to come; and he said concerning that book, that every jot and tittle thereof stood firmer than heaven and earth . . . Then I asked him further how I must make my supplication to him; and he said, Go and thou shalt find him upon a mercy-seat, where he sits all year long to give pardon and forgiveness to them that come. I told him that I knew not what to say when I came; and he bid me say to this effect: God be merciful to me a sinner, and make me to know and believe in Jesus Christ; for I see, that if his righteousness had not been, or I have not faith in that righteousness, I am utterly cast away. Lord, I have heard that thou art a merciful God, and hast ordained that thy Son Jesus Christ should be the Saviour of the world; and moreover, that thou art willing to bestow him upon a poor sinner as I am—and I am a sinner indeed. Lord, take therefore this opportunity and magnify thy grace in the salvation of my soul through thy Son Jesus Christ.' Bunyan says that Hopeful did not understand at once, but soon he did and said: 'From all which, I gathered that I must look for righteousness in his person, and for satisfaction for my sins by his blood; that what he did in obedience to his Father's law, and in submitting to the penalty thereof, was not for himself, but for him that will accept it for his salvation, and be thankful.'[4]

This is what 'believing on the Lord Jesus' means. If a man has believed in this way he has God's promise that he is a Christian.[5]

Of course, *becoming* a Christian is just the beginning, but we will think more about that in the last section of this book.

After a person has become a Christian, four things will help him:

1. A regular study of the Bible, which is God's communication to us.
2. Regular prayer. Now that our guilt has been removed, there is no barrier between us and God and we are able to talk freely with Him. There are two kinds of praying we shall need to practise: special times of prayer, and the constant looking to the Lord as we go about our daily tasks.
3. Talking to others about the God who exists and His solution to Man's dilemma.
4. Regular attendance at a church where the Bible is believed. This does not mean every church, but one that is true to the content of the Bible.

Pre-Evangelism: No Soft Option

CHAPTER I

Commending the Christian Faith
to our Generation

DEFENCE OF THE FAITH

There are two purposes of Christian apologetics. The first is defence. The second is to communicate Christianity in a way that any given generation can understand.

Defence is proper and necessary because in every age historic Christianity will be under attack. Defence does not mean being on the defensive. One must not be embarrassed about the use of the word *defence*. The proponents of any position who are alive to their own generation must give a sufficient answer for it when questions are raised about it. Thus, the word defence is not used here in a negative sense, because, in any conversation, in any communication which is really dialogue, answers must be given to objections raised.

Such answers are necessary in the first place for myself as a Christian, if I am going to maintain my intellectual integrity, and if I am to keep united my personal, devotional and intellectual life. In the second place, these answers are necessary for the sake of those for whom I have a responsibility.

It is unreasonable to expect people of the next generation in any age to continue in the historic Christian position, unless they are helped to see where arguments and connotations brought against Christianity and against them by their generation are fallacious. We must prepare Christian young people to face the monolithic twentieth-century culture by teaching them what the particular attack in our generation is, in contrast to the attacks of previous generations.

I find that everywhere I go—both in the United States and in other countries—children of Christians are being lost to historic Christianity. This is happening not only in small groups in small geographical areas but everywhere. They are being lost because their parents are unable to understand their children, and therefore they cannot really help them in their time of need. This lack of understanding is not only on the part of individual parents, but often also of churches, Christian colleges and Christian missions. Some Christian colleges (and I am not talking of 'liberal' colleges) lose many of the top ten per cent of their students before they graduate. We have left the next generation naked in the face of the twentieth-century thought by which they are surrounded.

So then, the defence, for myself and for those for whom I am responsible, must be a conscious defence. We cannot assume that, because we are Christians, in the full biblical sense, and indwelt by the Holy Spirit, automatically we shall be free from the influence of what surrounds us. The Holy Spirit can do what He will, but the Bible does not separate His work from knowledge; nor does the work of the Holy Spirit remove our responsibility as parents, pastors, evangelists, missionaries or teachers.

COMMUNICATION OF THE FAITH

Having said that, however, Christian apologetics should never stop at guarding against attack. We have a responsibility to communicate the Gospel to our generation.

Christian apologetics is not like living in a castle with the drawbridge up and occasionally tossing a stone over the walls. It is not to be based on a citadel mentality—sitting inside and saying, 'You cannot reach me here.' If the Christian adopts this attitude, either in theory or in practice, his contacts with those who have accepted twentieth-century thought will stop. Apologetics should not be merely an academic subject, a new kind of scholasticism. It should be thought out and practised in the rough and tumble of living contact with the present generation. Thus, the Christian should not be interested only in presenting a nicely balanced system on its own, like some Greek metaphysical system, but rather in something which has constant contact with reality—the reality of the questions being asked by his own generation.

No one can become a Christian unless he understands what Christianity is saying. Many pastors, missionaries and Christian teachers seem to be helpless as they try to speak to the educated people and the mass of people about them. They do not seem to face the fact that it is our task to speak to *our* generation; the past has gone, the future is not yet here. *So the positive side of apologetics is the communication of the Gospel to the present generation in terms that they can understand.*

It is important to remember, first of all, that we cannot separate true apologetics from the work of the Holy Spirit, nor from a living relationship in prayer to the Lord on the part of the Christian.

We must understand that eventually the battle is not just against flesh and blood.

However, the biblical emphasis that knowledge is needed prior to salvation will influence us in attaining that knowledge which is needed to communicate the Gospel. Historic Christianity has never separated itself from knowledge. It insists that all truth is one, and we must live and teach this even if twentieth-century thought and theology deny it.

The invitation to act comes only after an adequate base of knowledge has been given. This accords with the reason John gave for writing his Gospel: 'Many other signs therefore did Jesus in the presence of his disciples which are not written in this book. But these are written that ye may believe that Jesus is the Christ, the Son of God: and that believing ye may have life in his name.'[1] The word 'sign' is related to the historic events of the life, death and resurrection of Christ as put forth in this Gospel. In twentieth-century language we could translate 'sign' as 'space-time proof': 'Many other space-time proofs therefore did Jesus'. Note that these space-time proofs which, by their very nature, are observable were set forth as having been done in the presence of the disciples who observed them. And not only that, but that they have been written down in verbalised form. This means, of course, that these space-time proofs can be considered on the basis of the normal use of language as set forth in grammars and lexicons.

The order in these verses is important. Firstly, these are space-time proofs in written form, and consequently capable of careful consideration. Then, secondly, these proofs are of such a nature as to give good and sufficient evidence that Christ is the Messiah as prophesied in the Old Testament, and also that He is the Son of God. So that, thirdly, we are not asked to believe until we have faced the question as to whether this is true on the basis of the space-time evidence.

The same kind of groundwork of true knowledge is set forth in the Prologue of the gospel of Luke:[2] 'Forasmuch as many have taken in hand to draw up a narrative concerning those matters which have been fulfilled among us' (There are things which have happened in history, in the space-time before 'us'), 'even as they delivered them unto us, which from the beginning were eye witnesses' (This history is open to verification by eye witnesses) 'and ministers of the word, it seemed good to me also, having traced the course of all things accurately from the first, to write unto thee in order, most excellent Theophilus' (What is open to verification can also be communicated verbally in writing) 'that thou mightest know the truth concerning the

141

the things (or words) wherein thou wast instructed.' There is no leap in the dark, for it is possible to 'know the truth. Only when we have understood this introduction are we ready for the rest of the gospel of Luke, beginning in the next verse, 'There was in the days of Herod, King of Judaea, a certain priest . . .' We know from the Prologue that Luke is dealing with a framework of historic truth, and we are to place Herod, Zacharias and Christ within this space-time framework.

Knowledge precedes faith. This is crucial in understanding the Bible. *To say, as a Christian should, that only the faith which believes God on the basis of knowledge is true faith, is to say something which causes an explosion in the twentieth-century world.*

CHAPTER 2

The Importance of Truth

Some time ago I was speaking at Oxford University to a group of theological students on the subject of communicating the Gospel to those people who are particularly dominated by the consensus of twentieth-century thinking. When I had finished speaking, a Canadian post-graduate student stood up and said, 'Sir, if we understand you correctly, you are saying that pre-evangelism must come before evangelism. If this is so, then we have been making a mistake at Oxford. The reason we have not been reaching many of these people is because we have not taken enough time with pre-evangelism.' I said that I totally agreed.

TRUTH STANDS BEFORE CONVERSION

Before a man is ready to become a Christian, he must have a proper understanding of truth, whether he has fully analysed his coneept of truth or not. All people, whether they realise it or not, function in the framework of some concept of truth. Our concept of truth will radically affect our understanding of what it means to become a Christian. We are concerned, at this point, not with the *content* of truth, so much as with the *concept* of truth—what truth is.

Some who consider themselves real Christians have been infiltrated by the twentieth-century thought-forms. In reference to conversion, in a Christian sense, truth must be first. The phrase 'accepting Christ as Saviour' can mean anything. We are not saying what we are trying to say, unless we make completely clear that we are talking about objective truth, when we say Christianity is true and therefore that 'accepting Christ as Saviour' is not just some form of 'upper-storey leap'.

TRUTH AND SPIRITUALITY

Just as this matter of objective truth needs to be stressed before we can do effective evangelism, so the same thing must be considered before we can talk about true spirituality. From the biblical viewpoint, spirituality is not fragmented, and therefore it is to be contrasted to modern concepts of spirituality, both in the West and the East, and, unhappily, to some evangelical concepts. It is not fragmented because it concerns the whole man in his whole moment by moment life. Over against this true biblical view, some evangelicalism has been Platonic in the sense that too much emphasis has been put on the soul in contrast to the whole man including the body and the intellect.

It is very important to realise, over against modern concepts of spiritual experience, that the biblically based experience rests firmly on truth. It is not only an emotional experience, nor is it contentless.

We can think of true spirituality as having three parts. The indispensable beginning is to consider who (or what) 'is there', and how I can have a relationship to him (or it). That something must be understood and defined. You cannot have a personal relationship with something unknown. Then, having understood who it is with whom I am to have a personal relationship and how I may have it, comes the actual step of entering into that relationship. The Bible calls this being 'born again', and this is a step which a person can only take as an individual. We cannot be born again in groups, only one at a time. But to say that this is an individual matter is not the same as to say it is individualistic. The words may sound alike but they are worlds apart. This gives the basis for a whole sociological and cultural concept.

True spirituality cannot be abstracted from truth at one end nor from the whole man and the whole culture at the other. If there is a true spirituality, it must encompass all. The Bible insists that truth is one—and it is almost the sole surviving system in our generation that does.

To avoid confusion let us notice what this emphasis on the unity of truth does *not* involve. First of all, from the biblical viewpoint, truth is not ultimately related to orthodoxy. Orthodoxy is important and I am known as a man who is a convinced orthodox theologian. But truth is not ultimately related to orthodoxy. Secondly, truth is not related finally to the Creeds either. I, also, believe we must defend the historic Christian Creeds but, we must realise that, while the Creeds are important, truth is not finally related to them. Truth is related to something back of both orthodoxy and the Creeds.

Thirdly, truth is not ultimately related even to the Scriptures. Let me explain. Though I firmly believe what the Early Church and the Reformers taught concerning the nature of the Scriptures, and though I would emphasise that what they have to say concerning the Scriptures is crucially important, yet again, truth is finally related to something behind the Scriptures. The Scriptures are important, not because they are printed in a certain way nor bound in a certain kind of leather, nor because they have helped many people. This is not the basic reason for the Scriptures being overwhelmingly important. The Bible, the historic Creeds, and orthodoxy are important because God is there, and, finally, that is the only reason they have their importance.

The force of this was brought home to me several years ago when a young Swiss–German architect was reporting at one of our Farel House seminars in Switzerland on Max Planck's last essays. He pointed out that Planck, speaking in terms of his discipline, which was physics and not religion, said that modern man has had to move the screen back several times in our generation, and the question he posed was: what will be the final screen? Planck was saying that we do not know what the final screen will be in the material structure of the universe. This idea of a final screen started to bore away in my mind as a Christian, and as one speaking into the twentieth-century world. What is the final screen of truth?

The answer can only be the existence of God and who He is. Therefore Christian truth is that which is in relationship to what exists and ultimately to the God who exists. And true spirituality consists of being in the correct relationship to the God who is there, first in the once-for-all act of justification, secondly by being in that correct relationship as a continuing moment by moment reality. This is the biblical emphasis on true spirituality. It is a continuing moment by moment proper relationship to the God who exists.

THE GOD BEHIND TRUTH

I have chosen to use this expression 'God is there' as being equivalent to 'God exists', not because I am unaware of the theological discussions today, nor because I have met anyone who, holding to the truth of the Bible, believes in a three-storey universe; but in order to meet the problem of the new theology, which denies that God is there in the historical biblical sense. We must have the courage to say that God is there, or, to use different terminology, the final environment of what is there is God Himself, the one who has created everything else.

Let us notice carefully that, in saying God is there, we are saying God exists, and not just talking about the *word* god, or the *idea* god. We are speaking of the proper relationship to the living

God who exists. In order to understand the problems of our generation, we should be very alive to this distinction.

Semantics (linguistic analysis) makes up the heart of modern philosophical study in the Anglo-Saxon world. Though the Christian cannot accept this study as a total philosophy, there is no reason why he should not be glad for the concept that words need to be defined before they can be used in communication. As Christians we must understand that there is no word so meaningless as the word 'god' until it is defined. No word has been used to teach absolutely opposite concepts as much as the word 'god'. Consequently, let us not be confused. There is much 'spirituality' about us today that would relate itself to the *word* god or to the *idea* god; but this is not what we are talking about. Biblical truth and spirituality is not a relationship to the *word* god, or to the *idea* god. It is a relationship to the one who is there, which is an entirely different concept.

Following on from the discussion as to who or what God is, springs the second fundamental question of today, 'Who or what am I?' In order to make it possible to have a meaningful relationship between God and man, an answer to both questions must be given.

The answer we give here profoundly affects our idea of the form of the relationship between God and man. Whether we regard this relationship as mechanical, deterministic or—infinitely more wonderful—personal, will turn upon our answers to the questions 'Who is that God who is there?' and 'Who am I?'

Many sensitive people today are really struggling for their lives, asking the question, 'What is the purpose of man?' In fact, modern man has not come up with a satisfactory answer to this question, in any of his fields of thinking. It does not much matter whether he has approached it along the lines of naked rationalism or the leap into the dark of modern secular and theological mysticism; twentieth-century man has failed to answer this question.

When someone asks me the Christian answer to this question of purpose, the reason for man's existence, I would always take them to the first commandment of Christ. In passing, let us note that there is no reason to think that the first commandment: 'Thou shalt love the Lord thy God with all thy heart, and with all thy soul, and with all thy mind, and with all thy strength'[1] is merely a first commandment uttered by Jesus. We know it is not so because He quoted it from the last book of Moses, the book of Deuteronomy. But we can say something more. Surely it is the first commandment because it is the one that expresses the purpose of Man and, individually, my purpose.

But it is not enough to quote this on its own. Without the answer given by historic Christianity that God is really there, such an answer can only be another cliché to the honest enquirer, just one more twentieth-century 'religious answer'; and we cannot blame him if he stops listening. When I hear this first commandment to love the God who is there with everything that I am, it carries with it a total concept of life and of truth. A man can only love a God who exists and who is personal and about whom he has knowledge. So the fact that this God has communicated is also of supreme importance. But this commandment carries something more; it tells me something very fundamental and exciting about *myself*.

There is indeed something to be excited about if we know the dilemmas of our generation. If you could stand with me on the left bank of the Seine in Paris, or in the universities of Europe; if you could see the sober, sensitive men and women who come to our chalet asking these questions with real longings, you would realise there is something electrifying to know about 'myself'.

As far as the modern mentality is concerned, it is utterly shattering to be told that there is nothing intrinsically nonsensical in calling upon me to love the God who is there, and that God is of such a nature and that I am of such a nature as to make this a valid proposition. Those who understand what is involved will not dismiss this as 'something I have heard since I was little'. To think through the implications is totally exciting. The God who is there is of such a nature that He can be loved, and I am of such a nature that I can love; and thus this first commandment, or basic purpose of man, is the very opposite of a nonsense statement. I know what Man is, and I know who I am.

Personal and Corporate Living
into
The Twentieth Century Climate

CHAPTER I

Demonstrating the Character of God

SALVATION DOES NOT END WITH THE INDIVIDUAL

We have examined the tension which a non-Christian is bound to feel—the tension between the real world and the logical conclusion of a man's non-Christian presuppositions. If we are honest, Christians too, have a question to face. As people watch us, individually and corporately, and hear our presuppositions—what do they see with regard to our consistency to our presuppositions?

The man, now the Christian, and his presuppositions	⟶	The logical conclusion of our Christian presuppositions

In this concluding section I will try to pursue the question of a reality which is visible to a watching world.

As Christians, we must consider what are the logical conclusions of *our* presuppositions. Here we are speaking of apologetics, not abstractly, not scholastically, not as a subject taught in a Christian school, but as practised in the battles of our generation. Christian apologetics must be able to show intellectually that Christianity speaks of *true truth*; but it must also *exhibit* that it is not just a theory. This is needed for the defence of the flock of Christ, and also in the positive sense of reaching out to men who are honestly asking questions. What is observable, both individually and corporately, is also included in Christian apologetics. This should always have been comprehended and considered; but it is overwhelmingly important in view of the thought-forms of our generation to show that Christianity is not just a better dialectic.

We as orthodox evangelicals have often made the mistake of stopping with individual salvation. Historically the word Christian has meant two things. First, the word Christian defines a man who has accepted Christ as his Saviour. This is decidedly an individual thing. But there is a second consideration as well. It concerns what flows from individual salvation. While it is true that there is an individual salvation, and this is the beginning of the Christian life, yet nevertheless as we examine the teaching concerning the

Church and as we consider the Church at its strongest through the ages, that individual salvation should show itself also in *corporate* relationships.

When man fell, various divisions took place. The first and basic division is between man who has revolted and God. All other divisions flow from that. We are separated from God by our guilt — true moral guilt. Hence we need to be justified upon the basis of the finished substitutionary work of the Lord Jesus Christ. Yet it is quite plain from the Scriptures and from general observation that the separations did not stop with the separation of man from God. For, secondly, man was separated from himself. This gives rise to the psychological problems of life. Thirdly, man was separated from other men, leading to the sociological problems of life. Fourthly, man was separated from nature.

According to the teaching of the Scriptures, the finished work of the Lord Jesus Christ is meant eventually to bring healing to each of these divisions: healing which will be perfect in every aspect when Christ comes again in history in the future.

In justification, there is a relationship which is already perfect. When the individual accepts Christ as his Saviour, on the basis of the finished work of Christ, God as Judge declares that his guilt is gone immediately and for ever. In regard to the other separations, it is plain from the scriptural teaching and from the struggles of God's people throughout the good years of the Church, that in this life the blood of Christ is meant to bring *substantial* healing now. Individual salvation comes with justification and guilt is gone at once. Then comes a future day when my body will be raised from the dead, and the other separations will be just as completely healed. Now, in the present life, when men can observe us, there is to be a *substantial* healing of these other divisions. *Substantial* is the right word to use because it carries with it two ideas. Firstly, it means that it is not yet perfect. Secondly, it means that there will be reality.

THE VISIBLE QUALITY

The world has a right to look upon us and make a judgment. We are told by Jesus that as we love one another the world will judge, not only whether we are His disciples, but whether the Father sent the Son.[1] The final apologetic, along with the rational, logical defence and presentation, is *what the world sees* in the individual Christian and in our corporate relationships together. The command that we should love one another surely means something much richer than merely organisational relationship. Not that we should minimise proper organisational relationship, but one may look at men bound together in an organised group called a church and see nothing of a substantial healing of the division between men in the present life.

On the other hand, Jesus' teaching and the New Testament Church make plain that while there is 'the invisible Church', yet the Church is not to be hidden away, in an unseen area, as though it does not matter what men see. What we are called to do, upon the basis of the finished work of Christ in the power of the Spirit through faith, is to exhibit a substantial healing, individual and then corporate, so that men may observe it. Here too is a portion of the apologetic: a presentation which gives at least some demonstration that these things are neither theoretical nor a new dialectic, but real; not perfect, yet substantial. If we only speak of and exhibit the individual effects of the Gospel, the world, psychologically conditioned as it is today, will explain them away. What the world cannot explain away will be a substantial, corporate exhibition of the logical conclusions of the Christian presuppositions. It is not true that the New Testament presents an individualistic concept of salvation. Individual, yes: we must come one at a time; but it is not individualistic only. First there must be the individual reality, and then the corporate. Neither will be perfect in this life, but they must be real. I have discovered that hard twentieth-century people do not expect Christians to be perfect. They do not throw it in our teeth when, individually or corporately, they find less than perfection in us. They do not expect perfection, but they do expect reality; and they have a right to expect reality, upon the authority of Jesus Christ.

There must be communion and community among the people of God: not a false community, that is set up as though human community were an end in itself; but in the local church, in a mission, in a school, wherever it might be, there true fellowship must be evident as the outcome of original, individual salvation. This is the real Church of the Lord Jesus Christ—not merely organisation, but a group of people, individually the children of God, drawn together by the Holy Spirit for a particular task either in a local situation or over a wider area. The Church of the Lord Jesus should be a group of those who are redeemed and bound together on the basis of true doctrine. But subsequently they should show together a substantial 'sociological healing' of the breaches between men which have come about because of the results of man's sin.

The Christian sociological position is that the sociological problems which we find, regardless of what they may be, are a result of the separation that has come between men because of sin. Now the world should be able to see in the Church those marks which exhibit that there is a substantial sociological healing possible in the present generation. We can never expect the testimony of a previous generation to be sufficient for our own time. We can point to the wonders of past achievements, but men have a right to say, 'This is our moment, this is our history, what about today?' It is not enough for the Church to be engaged with the State in healing social ills, though this is important at times. But when the world can turn around and see a group of God's people exhibiting substantial healing in the area of human relationships in their present life, then the world will take notice. Each group of Christians is, as it were, a pilot plant, showing that something can be done in the present situation, if only we begin in the right way.

Corporate living in the early Church was very strong at this point. It was not perfect, but it was strong. The testimony has come down to us that one of the things that shook the Roman Empire was that as they looked upon these Christians—a cross section of the wide sociological spectrum in the Roman Empire from slaves to their masters, and including some of Caesar's household—non-Christians were forced to say, 'behold how they love each other', not in a vacuum, but loving each other in the circle of truth.

REALISM IN EXHIBITION

We must look to the Son of God, moment by moment, for these things; such things cannot be done in our own strength. We must allow Him to bear His fruit through us. We can proclaim 'orthodoxy' in the flesh, and we can compromise in the flesh. But our calling is a different calling: it is to exhibit God and His character, by His grace, in this generation. We need to show Him forth as personal, as holy and as love. It is possible in the flesh to be both orthodox and dead—or loving and compromising. What is not possible in the flesh is simultaneously to exhibit both the justice of God and the love of God—this can only be done through the work of the Holy Spirit. And yet anything less is not a picture of God, but only a caricature of the God who exists.

Demonstrating God's character must be existential. The existentialists are right at this place, though they are wrong when they say that history is not going anywhere. As far as living is concerned, we are on the knife-edge of time. What will matter is our relationship to the Lord Jesus, individually and then corporately, at this existential moment. What counts, as men look upon us individually and corporately, is whether we are exhibiting God and His character *now*. The Christian position is not static, but is living.

Christ says, 'Be ye therefore perfect, even as your Father which is in heaven is perfect.'[2] How could a perfect God say, 'Just sin a little bit'? This would be impossible. The standard is God's own perfection. And yet the Word of God does not leave us with a romantic notion that we must either have total perfection in this life or that we must smash everything and have nothing. I am firmly convinced that many wonderful things have been destroyed because people have had a preconceived and romantic notion in their minds as to what the perfect thing should be, would settle for nothing else, and thus have smashed what could have been.

How glad we should be for the Apostle John when he says, 'My little children, these things write I unto you, that ye sin not. And if any man sin, *we* have an advocate with the Father.'[3] There is a tremendous and wonderful implication in that word *we*. John, the beloved apostle, places himself among us. On the one hand, we must stand against all standards lower than perfection. The standards are not arbitrary, but are those which the holy God who exists has given us in the Bible, and we are to take them with total seriousness. Anything less than the totality of these standards will not do. Sin is not to be minimised either in the individual or the corporate life. Antinomianism in theory or practice is always wrong and destructive.

Yet on the other hand we must stand against all the romantic concepts of perfection in this life. The Bible does not promise us perfection in this life, except in the area of justification. It does not promise us in this life perfection morally, physically, psychologically or sociologically. There are to be moral victories and growth, but that is different from perfection. John could say 'we'. Paul could indicate his own lack of perfection.[4] There can be physical healing, but that does not mean that the one healed is then a perfect physical specimen. The day Lazarus was raised from the dead he may have had a headache and certainly one day he died again. People can be wonderfully helped psychologically, but that does not mean that they will then be totally integrated personalities. The Christian position is understanding that on this side of the resurrection the call *is* to perfection, and yet at the same time not to smash and destroy what we cannot bring again to life—just simply because it is less than the perfections that we romantically build in our thinking. For example, how many women have I found—and how many men—who have jumped on a perfectly good marriage until it was dead, just because they had a romantic concept of what marriage should or could be, either physically or emotionally.

PERSONALITY IS CENTRAL

We have been speaking about that which is vitally important in regard to the logical conclusions of the Christian presuppositions. So far we have spoken about the *corporate* and the *substantial*. Now we will add the third word: the *personal*.

The Christian system is consistent as no other system that has ever been. It is beautiful beyond words, because it has that quality that no other system completely has—you begin at the beginning, and you can go to the end. It is as simple as that. *And every part and portion of the system can be related back to the beginning.* Whatever you discuss, to understand it properly, you just go back to the beginning and the whole thing is in its place. The beginning is simply that God exists and that He is the personal-infinite God. Our generation longs for the reality of personality but it cannot find it. But Christianity says personality is valid because personality has not just appeared in the universe but rather is rooted in the personal God who has always been.

All too often, when we are talking to the lost world, we do not begin at the beginning and therefore the world stops listening. Without this emphasis on personality we cannot expect men really to listen, because without this the concept of salvation is hung in a vacuum.

If we understand this, we understand the meaning of life. The meaning of life does not end with justification, but is seen in the reality that when we accept Christ as our Saviour in the true biblical sense, our personal relationship with the personal God is restored. Every place we turn in Christianity we find that we are brought face to face with the wonder of personality—the very opposite of the dilemma and the sorrow of modern man who finds no meaning in personality. Consider the words of Paul, 'The grace of the Lord Jesus Christ, and the love of God, and the communion [and in the French the word is *communication*] of the Holy Ghost be with you all.'[5] It is the personal to which we are brought. First of all there is the personal relationship with God Himself—this is the most wonderful, and is not just in heaven but is substantially real in practice now. When we understand our calling it is not only true but beautiful—and it should be exciting. It is hard to understand how an orthodox, evangelical, Bible-believing Christian can fail to be excited. The answers in the realm of the intellect should make us overwhelmingly excited. But much more than this, we are returned to a personal relationship with the God who is there. If we are unexcited Christians we should go back and see what is wrong. We are surrounded by a generation that can find 'no one home' in the universe. If anything marks our generation it is this. In contrast to this, as a Christian I know who I am; and I know the personal God who is there. I speak and He hears. I am not surrounded by mere mass, nor only energy particles, but He is there. And if I have accepted Christ as my Saviour, then though it will not be perfect in this life, yet moment by moment, on the basis of the finished work of Christ, this person to person relationship with the God who is there can have reality to me.

CHAPTER 2

The Legal, but not only the Legal

Today most non-Christians exclude any real notion of Law. They do this because they have no *absolute* anywhere in the universe, and without any absolute one really cannot have any morals as morals. For them, everything is relative; they have no real *circle* of Law. For them there is no circle inside which there is right, in contrast to that which is outside the circle and therefore wrong. To the Christian this is not so. God does exist and He has a character; there are things which are outside the commandments He has given us as the expression of His character. For example, there is therefore a proper legal circle in regard to the visible Church. The visible Church should be a true Church. It will not be a perfect Church, but it should be a true one. And marriage is the proper circle for sexual relationships. The new morality, following the new theology and lacking the Christian epistemology, the Christian Scripture and the Christian God, can find no real legal circle and so finds no way to set boundaries.

The fault of orthodoxy is that though it has a legal circle it tends too often to act as though merely to be within the circle is enough. We should be thankful for the legal circle—a real absolute, something we can know and within which we can function— because it means that we do not have to act on the assumption that we can weigh all the results of our acts out to infinity, when, being finite, we cannot see the results of our acts more than one or two steps ahead. Having to act as a finite god is painful. But what a tragedy to think that because we are in the proper legal circle everything is finished and done—as though marriage, the Church, and other human relationships are static and that only the legal circle is important.

Even in justification many Christians who are perfectly orthodox in doctrine look back upon their justification as though it were the end of all, at least until death comes. It is not so. Birth is essential to life but the parent is not glad only for the birth of his child. He is thankful for the living child that grows up. Whoever saw a young couple get engaged simply because they wanted to enjoy the marriage ceremony? What they want to do is to live together. So it is with becoming a Christian. In one way you can say that the new birth is everything; in another way you can say that really it is very little. It is everything, because it is indispensable to begin with, but it is little in comparison with the living existential relationship. The legal circle of justification does not end statically; it opens to me a living person-to-person communication, with the God who exists.

In marriage, in the Church and in other human relationships the same thing applies—the proper legal relationship must be there, but if it is static it becomes a dusty monument. It is no longer beautiful. It becomes a flower that dies under a glass. It can only be beautiful if inside the proper legal circle we have a personal relationship which speaks of the personal God who is there. This is our calling, not only to exhibit something substantially real to a watching world, but as a joy to the Christian himself. I am called to love God with all my heart and soul and mind, and I am called to love my neighbour as myself: each man in the proper circle and in the proper relationship.

If we say that personality is not an intrusion in the universe but central, the world has a right to see the Christians both individually and corporately living on a personal level. Men must see that we take personality seriously enough, by the grace of God, to act upon it.

There must be an observable indication of this in the midst of the daily life in this present abnormal world, or we have denied the central Christian presupposition.

HUMAN PEOPLE IN OUR CULTURE

When we use the phrase, 'it is only human', we are usually referring to something sinful. In this sense, the Christian should feel a calling *not* to be 'human'; but in a more profound sense, the Christian is called to exhibit the characteristics of true humanity, because being a man is not intrinsically being sinful man, but being that which goes back before the Fall, to man made in the image of God. Therefore Christians in their relationships should be the most *human* people you will ever see. This speaks for God in an age of inhumanity and impersonality and facelessness. When people look at us their reaction should be, 'These are human people'; human, because we know that we differ from the animal, the plant and the machine; and that personality is native to what has always been.

If they cannot look upon us and say, 'They are real people', nothing else is enough. Far too often young people become Christians and then search among the Church's ranks for real people, and have a hard task finding them. All too often evangelicals are paper people.

If we do not preach these things, talk about them to each other, and teach them carefully from the pulpit and in the Christian classroom, we cannot expect Christians so to act. This has always been important, but it is especially so today because we are surrounded by a world in which personality is increasingly eroded. If we, who have become God's children, do not show Him to be personal in our lives, then in practice we are denying His existence and He cannot be anything but grieved. Man should see a beauty among Christians in their practice of the centrality of personal relationships. This is equivalent today, when many think both Man and God are dead, to the songs of wonder and exultation in the Old Testament, sung because God is a living God and not a lifeless idol.

PERSONALITY AND CULTURE

It seems to me that there are three ways of understanding and judging a work of art. (I mean here art in the widest sense.) The first thing to consider is its *technical excellence*. This stands as a thing by itself. The second thing is to consider its *validity*. By this I mean the honesty of the work of art in expressing what the artist really thinks. For Salvador Dali with his world-view to give the same expression as Rembrandt would be invalid. Therefore, as I view a work of art expressing a non-Christian message, I do not need to take it, cast it to the ground and say it is nothing, and so walk upon the personality of the man who made it. In the technical aspects and in the validity as important things in themselves, I can meet the man openly as a man, and deal with him on the basis of the importance of personality.

Now I can turn to the third way to judge a work of art: its *message*. I am not shut up to the two impossible alternatives of dealing with the work of art as nothing, and thus walking upon the person who produced it; or on the other hand, judging its message on the false base of synthesis. I can say its message is wrong and destructive, that it sends men into despair. Yet at the same time I can deal with empathy with the man who produced it and draw attention to his technical excellence and integrity. Looking at him as a person, I may be sorry because he is in the midst of despair and teaching others despair, and I may stand strongly against his message; but I am not taking him as a personality and beating him into the dust as though he were less than man made in the image of God. It is possible to reject the message on the basis of truth or moral absolutes without implying by this that we have nothing to say to him as a man in appreciation of what he, as a man, has produced in art, engineering or whatever it is. As an artist, the technical excellence may be high, it may even be to the level of genius. His validity may be high as well. I am still dealing with him in integrity as a personality, even though I must take that book or painting and say the message is destruction and death.

Christianity touches all of life, Christ is Lord of the whole life of the Christian. Culture and education should neither be viewed as neutral nor yet as outside the Christian's interest. Christians are to be whole people and, especially if our educational institutions are to be honest in education, we must open the doors with integrity to the works of art and knowledge of men. What we have been speaking of is the way to open the doors wide without, on the one hand, destroying those we teach nor, on the other hand, disgusting them because we are not fair to men as men.

We are not confined in families, educational institutions, churches or missions—to only two alternatives: either a heterodoxy, a lowering of the lines, a drift to synthesis; or the equally horrible alternative of deadness, without interest in personality, joy and beauty. Why should we be, when neither of these alternatives reflect what man is as man or what God is? The *message* of an artist or teacher is to be judged on the basis of truth and the biblical moral absolutes, and the Christian and the Christian institution must make it plain that being an artist does not exempt a man from being a creature and thus under the Law of God.

However, no matter how rebellious he may be he does not cease to be a man, and therefore we must in no circumstance treat him as less. Christian education in the family, the church and the school, if it is to be true (or even useful to its generation) must always *consciously* be wrestling with these two things: truth which is not exhaustive but propositionally true (in contrast to a dialectical methodology and synthesis); and simultaneously the exhibition of the personal.

On the final day of a series of lectures I was giving at a Christian College in America, the president of the Student Council handed me the following letter written on Student Council stationery:

'Dear Dr. Schaeffer,

'You have helped me a great deal this week, to spot some of the reasons for my rebellion against both the evangelical form of ortho-doxy, and to some degree against God. For this I can't thank you enough, nor can I thank God enough for helping me to see myself a little more clearly. The difficulty, of course, comes in the implementation of my conclusions into my own being, though I trust this will occur.

'I am also concerned about the effect that your messages may have on the rest of the campus and on evangelicalism as a whole. You have asserted that Christianity is both a system, orthodoxy, and a personal association with Christ. As such there are some absolutes which we as Christians can depend on and demand of others if they are to be considered truly Christian. With this I agree, although I may not hold to all the absolutes which you have indicated are necessary for the Christian "system". But the matter which is of concern to me is that there are many here at (— — —) and in evangelicalism who, because they believe they have true truth, impose their own societal and evangelical, subcultural absolutes on those of us who have had "the roof blown off". The result is that students are often forced into either accepting evangelicalism, with all of its absolutes, be they Victorian or early twentieth-century, or out into total despair. Believe me, sir, when I say there are many at (— — —) in this position. In fact, this is what has finally driven many into Neo-orthodoxy and scepticism.

'This brings me to my final point which is simply this: Now that you have succeeded in "blowing the roof off" for some students, and have instructed evangelicalism to go and do likewise, would you please tell us how evangelicalism can eliminate some of these extraneous absolutes which make orthodoxy (as we know it) almost impossible to swallow. How can evangelicals really become the salt of the earth when many of their absolutes forbid them to even come into contact with the earth ? How does the evangelical house clean out enough dust to make it the orthodox house, and then perhaps we will be relevant to the twentieth-century man?

Very Sincerely (— — —)
Student Council President.'

I do not think that I would agree with this student in all the details involved, but I do agree that there is much dust to clear out. Our task is to deal with the dust, but not to burn down the house in order to remove it.

Appendices

The Problem of the Middle-Class Church in the Latter Half of the Twentieth Century

It is my hope that this book may be useful in helping orthodox evangelicalism so that it will be a thing of strength and beauty in the second half of the twentieth century.

In order for evangelicalism to be this, three principles must be observed:

1. The full doctrinal position of historic Christianity must be clearly maintained.
2. Every honest question must be given an honest answer. It is unbiblical for anyone to say, 'just believe'.
3. There must be an individual and corporate exhibition that God exists in our century, in order to show that historic Christianity is more than just a superior dialectic or a better point of psychological integration.

There are two sections of our society to which, by and large, we are failing to communicate—the intellectuals on the one hand and the workers on the other. The problem of being largely middle-class in our churches becomes really pressing both because of this, and also when we realise that we are losing many of the children of Christian parents because they no longer accept their middle-class background in either home or local church.

In the two increasingly important areas of ideas and the application of morals, the vast majority of churches have little to say either to intellectuals or workers or, too often, to the young people from Christian homes.

Working in Switzerland we have had many Christians' children who are honestly confused, coming from many different countries. They find so often that the answers they have been given simply do not touch the problems which are *their* problems. But this observation is gleaned not only from the many people who come to us in Switzerland, but also from travelling over much of the Western world, lecturing in many different places.

It is therefore my considered opinion that if the Church today is really concerned to break out of its middle-class format and meet the intellectuals, workers and young people where they are, it must make an honest and courageous attempt to implement all three of the principles above. It is as we who are working together in L'Abri Fellowship have sought by the grace of God, even though totally inadequately, to put them into practice, that we have seen many twentieth-century men and women reached by the Gospel. It would be our conclusion that all three points are imperative, wherever the Church is serious in wanting to speak to these of our generation.

We do not think that this material and outlook is shut up to a few exotic Christian works dealing with the international intellectual and creative people. A number of those who have spent time to grasp this material are now using it with the uneducated with worthwhileness. For this we are thankful.

But even more, we are convinced that a proper use of this comprehension and material would be helpful also within the 'middle-class' churches and institutions which make up so much of evangelicalism and orthodoxy today. Firstly, it would give a new dimension of wealth in Christ to those churches, missions, and institutions. Secondly, it would be much harder for those round about to write them off as a sub-culture, representing largely only yesterday. Thirdly, they could protect their own next generation. The Christians have been in danger not only of not understanding, but of not taking seriously the problems of their children.

I must say that I am deeply troubled not only by what I find amongst our own Western churches, but also by what I come up against among Christian converts from overseas. On many occasions as I have been lecturing to international groups in England and elsewhere, I have felt torn to bits for those from overseas who have been educated in mission schools and then sent out naked into the twentieth-century world.

The work of the Holy Spirit should never be minimised, but nowhere in the Scriptures do we find the work of the Holy Spirit an excuse for laziness and lack of love on the part of those with Christian responsibility. Nor is the Holy Spirit ever old-fashioned in the bad meaning of that term.

A word of warning here. To grasp and apply the principles we have been seeking to lay down is not just to memorise a static framework or terminology; this could be just one more dead thing.

One of the joys in our work is to see how many young people and more mature teachers are carrying this thinking into their own academic disciplines and the arts, and are developing them along the lines of their own fields of interest.

As we seek to meet the problems there are two things which we must strenuously seek to avoid, whether we are engaged in teaching, missionary work, or in some aspect of the life of the local church.

First, settling down and accepting the present situation simply because of the inertia caused by those who speak of the problem of the churches' young people and speak much of missions, but who simply do not want to question the familiar because it is painful to do so. The problem is that the evangelical, orthodox churches, institutions and programmes, are today often under the control of those who are in this category. This control is both organisational and financial. Thus, there is a tendency not to 'rock-the-boat'. This responsibility cannot be met by the young people themselves, nor by the young ministers and young missionaries alone.

Mature Christians must summon the courage to distinguish, under the Holy Spirit, between unchangeable biblical truth and the things which have only become comfortable for us. Often one hears people speak of 'the simple Gospel only', when in reality they do not really care enough for those outside the churches, or their own children for that matter, to be willing to face what preaching the simple Gospel may mean in a changing and complex situation.

Second, the development of an intellectual and cultural snobbishness. This can easily come about unless we help one another not to fall into it. Such an attitude grieves the Holy Spirit, destroys rather than builds and is as offensively ugly as anything can be.

We will make mistakes, but by God's grace we must strive to avoid either of these two errors or a choice between them.

After considerable thought and the practical experience of trying it out in several countries, I would suggest the following two concepts be borne in mind as we train our young people to take their full part in the Christian work of our time.

First of all, it must be remembered that those who make up the body of the churches and the institutions are also the lambs of God. They need care and help just as much as do the intellectual, the creative people and the young people who are becoming twentieth-century people. When a pastor accepts the call to go to a particular church, his call is to minister to the whole congregation. It is simple honesty to keep in mind that his salary is being contributed to by all. Those who care nothing about the new problems are yet to be fed and shepherded. Therefore, the general preaching and teaching in the middle-class evangelical church should not be of such a nature as to confuse, hurt or undernourish them.

On the other hand, nothing should be preached or taught in the general services and classes which will have to be unlearned when young people and others read and discuss the deeper problems or go away to university. I would suggest that all Sunday School, Bible Class and educational material should be prepared with this in mind. We should ask ourselves the question, 'Is the material of such a nature that it could be extended by eighteen years of honest study without it proving false?'

This will mean more attention to the preparation of sermons, lesson material, Bible-study notes and so on. Not everyone will be equally adapted to do this, but each could be helped if Christian schools, seminaries and theological colleges, Bible schools, missionary training institutes and publishing houses, would set up a programme in order to avoid making the old mistakes and omissions and would add some to their staff who had been trained to think in a total cultural apologetic. The programme could be set up to be operative at a given date, say in three years' time. Let us remind ourselves, all this began culturally in the United States in a larger way at the time of the Armory Show in New York in 1913. Thus, we have had fifty years. And since the major shift in the United States between 1930 and 1940, in all the major denominations, and from a Reformation-based culture to the post-Christian culture, we have had over twenty-five years. In England and on the Continent there has been even more time.

Thus, my first suggestion would be: the general teaching and preaching should be of such a nature as to feed and care for those who make up the body of the congregation or institution, yet keeping in mind that nothing is given which must be unlearned as deeper problems are later met.

Second, I would suggest that special times be set aside in the church, institution or mission, where those who are in, or are coming into, the twentieth-century problems can get what they need. The occasion could be a talk, discussion or seminar. It would be valuable if those claiming no affiliation to the Church could be brought into the discussion as well. It does not have to be a big gathering or extensively publicised, but rather the gathering together of those in the Church and outside the Church who wish to get on. Nor does this getting on have to be purely intellectual, for if one goes deep enough into the intellectual questions one comes to the deep spiritual problems and realities, just as when one goes deep enough spiritually one touches on the real intellectual problems and realities.

Men and women trained in this way will then have the opportunity, as they go overseas or into unfamiliar territories at home, of understanding what are the twentieth-century problems men face.

So it would seem to me that a course in homiletics or apologetics which does not consciously seek to implement these two suggestions is really today a preparation for failure and sorrow.

Christian conferences, etc. could have a place for caring for these considerations on a deeper and extended level. Surely too, those who have a responsibility for Christian radio programmes could at least find small corners for those who, in many places, make up the majority of the population.

In this way all could be fed, and if introduced not too rapidly, with much emphasis on spiritual growth and love as well as understanding, in most cases there would not have to be two 'churches' under one roof, nor an explosion.

Yet I would say that some ripples are worthwhile rather than allowing those outside, and our own young people who are longing for real answers, to choke in the all-too-present dustiness.

The Practice of Truth

In regard to the first of the principles of which we spoke at the beginning of Appendix A: *The full doctrinal position of historic Christianity must be clearly maintained,* it would seem to me that the central problem of evangelical orthodoxy in the second half of the twentieth century is the problem of the *practice* of this principle. This is especially so when we take into account the spiritual and intellectual mentality which is dominant in our century. Any consideration of methods and programmes is secondary to a consideration of this central problem.

If a clear and unmistakable emphasis on truth, in the sense of antithesis, is removed, two things occur: firstly, Christianity in the next generation as true Christianity is weakened; and secondly, we shall be communicating only with that diminishing portion of the community which still thinks in terms of the older concept of truth. We are not minimising the work of the Holy Spirit. We would remember, however, that our responsibility is so to communicate that those who hear the Gospel will understand it. If we do not communicate clearly on the basis of antithesis, many will respond to their own interpretation of the Gospel, in their own relativistic thought-forms, including a concept of psychological guilt feelings rather than of true moral guilt before the holy, living God. If they do respond in this way, they have not understood the Gospel; they are still lost, and we have defaulted in our task of preaching and communicating the Gospel to our generation.

The unity of orthodox or evangelical Christianity should be centred around this emphasis on *truth.* It is always important, but doubly so when we are surrounded by so many for whom the concept of truth, in the sense of antithesis, is considered to be totally unthinkable.

In such a setting the problem of communication is serious; it can only be overcome by negative statements that clearly say what we do *not* mean; so that the twentieth-century man understands the positive statements we *do* mean. Moreover, in an age of synthesis, men will not take our protestations of truth seriously unless they see by our actions that we seriously *practise* truth and antithesis in the unity we try to establish and in our activities. Without this, in an age of relativity, we cannot expect the evangelical, orthodox Church to mean much to the surrounding culture or even to the Church's own children, for what we try to say in our teaching and evangelism will be understood in the twentieth-century thought-form of synthesis. Both a clear comprehension of the importance of truth and a clear practice of it, even when it is costly to do so, is imperative if our witness and our evangelism are to be significant in our own generation and in the flow of history.

It would seem to me that some evangelicals are jettisoning any serious attempt to exhibit truth and antithesis. There has been a tendency to move from a lack of seriousness ecclesiastically concerning truth to the same tendency in matters of wider co-operation. This often finishes up by denying, in practice if not in theory, the importance of doctrinal truth as such.

Many evangelicals who are rightly disturbed by the new theology's view of the Scriptures and universalism and who try to meet it at these points of error in fact never go far enough back in order to establish a clear line of truth and error which will hold the weight for the next generation. Inevitably the next generation tends to go further in the direction already established and , if this is already moving towards synthesis, they will move with it ever closer to the new theology. Therefore, to avoid this, we must be careful to consider what truth and antithesis mean *in practice* in ecclesiastical matters and in evangelism.

Thus it must be said that in spite of (and even because of) one's commitment to evangelism and co-operation among Christians, I can visualise times when the only way to make plain the seriousness of what is involved in regard to a service or an activity where the Gospel is going to be preached is *not* to accept an official part, if men whose *doctrine* is known to be an enemy are going to be invited to officially participate. In an age of relativity the *practice* of truth when it is costly is the only way to cause the world to take seriously our protestations concerning truth. Co-operation and unity that do not lead to purity of life and purity of doctrine are just as faulty and incomplete as an orthodoxy which does not lead to a concern for, and a reaching out towards, those who are lost.

There is an opposite danger to be avoided. Some of those who have contended for truth have cut the ground from under this position, not only by a loss of beauty and love but even, in practice, by a loss of truth in speaking about men.

All too often the only antithesis we have exhibited to the world and to our own children has been our *talking* about holiness *or* our *talking* about love; rather than the consideration and practice of holiness and love together as truth, in antithesis to what is false in theology, in the church, and the surrounding culture.

A Word Concerning L'Abri

by

The Rev. J. A. Kirk, B.D., B.A., A.K.C.
Professor of New Testament at the Union Theological
Seminary, Buenos Aires

Dr. Schaeffer and his wife were paying one of their periodic visits to Cambridge when I first met them. It was the beginning of the summer term 1963, my last term at theological college. Many of us who were concerned with the communication of the Christian faith were at that moment much perplexed by the recent spate of thought, known popularly as the 'New Cambridge Theology'. A group of eminent theologians had tried in a book called *Soundings*, published in 1962, to rethink the meaning of Christianity in the light of an increasing rejection of it by secular thinkers. In the previous term four of the dons then teaching in the university theological faculty had given a series of lectures under the title 'Objections to Christian Belief', each of which had attracted a large audience of undergraduates. And then in March of that year as a kind of crowning achievement a former Cambridge scholar, Dr. John Robinson, had popularised much modern theological thinking from his bed of sickness. The word 'ferment' had been added to the ecclesiastical repertoire of approved words and debate on these matters became intense and vociferous.

My own field of theological study has been concentrated in the area of the New Testament, and I felt generally ill-prepared to think through many of the more philosophical conclusions which should have resulted from that contemporary rash of writing. I was convinced, in my own limited way, of the veracity of the Bible as God's sufficient communication to men. I knew about enough of modern New Testament studies to be highly dubious of the results of much of it that claimed to be objective and scientific in approach. For I was largely unable to see by what *substantial* canons of criticism many of the sceptical German and English New Testament scholars worked. It seemed to me that much of what was often uncritically accepted as the sure results of critical scholarship was no more than baseless speculation. Therefore I saw no reason to accept that there were any really *conclusive* grounds for asserting that the Bible was riddled with error. That was roughly the point I had reached in trying to wrestle with modern critical theology. The recent upsurge of Cambridge theological writing seemed to me destructive and empty and lacking any real answer to the intellectual and moral gropings of the modern generation. Indeed it may well be that none of these writers would have considered they had the ability to give such answers. On the other hand I was none too happy that the current evangelical approach to this modern debate was really satisfactory, either as a defence of biblical Christianity or as a means of helping out of their impasse the majority of modern people, trapped as they were within their non-Christian frameworks. There was and is an unhealthy form of evangelicalism which seeks to dismiss opposing views as insincere and even ungodly without really providing a reasonable alternative.

From the point of view of the then current debate Dr. Schaeffer's visit was timely and helpful. Those of us who listened to him talking about *Honest to God*, whether we agreed with him or not, and some present would not have, nevertheless had to admit that we were hearing what appeared to be an entirely fresh approach from the evangelical standpoint. What impressed me about what he said was not so much that he tried to answer the book point by point as that he demonstrated how it fitted into the complex history of modern thought and culture, non-theological as well as theological. In other words we were given a panoramic sweep of the last two hundred years or so of Western and Eastern thinking rather than a microscopic view of one man's ideas. Obviously I would not want to imply by this that Dr. Schaeffer covered everything that could be covered in the course of only one lecture and discussion, but that he succeeded along broad lines in relating the modern theological debate, as exemplified in these books, to the total culture of our modern world, even tracing it back as far as the Renaissance.

This was something I had never heard an evangelical doing before and to me it had exciting possibilities in the total witness to biblical truth. I would hazard a guess that the way in which Dr. Schaeffer himself became a Christian has very much controlled the way he understands these things today.

During the next three years as I listened further to some of Dr. Schaeffer's lectures on tape and also heard him from time to time in London, I began to realise that we had, amongst those of us who accepted the inerrancy of Scripture, a man to whom God had given a special gift of understanding the mentality of the twentieth century and of identifying himself with people affected by it. He had been led to a position where at one and the same time he could brilliantly expose this mentality and yet also sympathetically find ways of giving the only answers which could possibly satisfy man's deepest longings for order and reality in their lives.

My growing interest in what Dr. Schaeffer was saying and the way God was leading him, his family and the community which was growing up in Switzerland led me to visit them in the summer of 1966 and to do some further study.

The centre of the work is in a little village about three thousand feet above the Rhône valley. It is one of those villages you might easily pass through without noticing on your way to a 'popular' Swiss resort; for the road on which it is situated leads to a famous ski centre.

Twelve years ago the Schaeffers began in one chalet their work of seeking to explain to all whom God sent them the wonderful answers which the Christian faith gives to all man's greatest dilemmas. The first person who came was a young American girl then studying with one of the Schaeffers' daughters in the University of Lausanne. After a long absence she returned in 1966 having won a hard battle to maintain her Christian faith.

Since then hundreds of people, mostly young, but by no means exclusively so, have ascended the steep mountain road and found the warm friendship and welcome of the L'Abri family—for that is the name by which the community is called. The people who arrive at L'Abri have come from many parts of the world and by diverse routes.

A young Greek student studying philosophy at a European university was standing in front of Lausanne Cathedral looking lost when a German girl who was studying at L'Abri met her. Though unmarried she was expecting a child and had nowhere to turn. Though she had no idea what to expect, she accepted an invitation to stay with the Schaeffers and was more than surprised to learn on arriving that L'Abri was a place where philosophic answers on the basis of the Christian faith were given to people's problems. She stayed six months, had her baby and was seen through the legal necessities surrounding this.

A number of young people from a school in Geneva had spent week-ends at L'Abri before the principal of the school forbade any further visits. One of these was a young American boy who, during one of the week-ends, had professed faith in Jesus Christ. Having no Christian background he did not know where to find a Bible-believing Church back in America and as a result of discovering only 'liberal' churches soon drifted off into the by-ways of non-Christian sectarian movements. Eventually he became

173

fascinated by Hinduism and this led in time to a journey by boat to India in order to study it at the most fundamental level possible. However, during the trip he was reminded of L'Abri and something of what he had learnt during his short time there. Consequently he prayed that God might reveal the true path to Himself. Almost immediately he came across some missionaries travelling to India on the same boat. The outcome of this meeting was to give up his interest in Hinduism and make a direct flight from Bombay to Geneva from where he travelled to L'Abri and studied at Farel House for about a year.

Many instances of the remarkable circumstances which have brought people to visit or study in this tiny Swiss village could be multiplied many times and each one would involve a fascinating story. The workers at L'Abri are convinced that one thing is true of every individual who comes and that is that God has sent them in answer to specific, earnest prayer.

The people who come are not only different in backgrounds of nationality and colour, such as Japanese and Dutch, African and German, Indian and English, South African, American, South Korean and many more, but also in beliefs. There are atheists, agnostics, existentialists, those from a Hindu background, committed and uncommitted Jews, Roman Catholics, Liberal Protestants, Buddhists, and many more who have accepted the relativistic thinking of the twentieth century. For the most part all of these who come are unhappy in their views and are longing for real substantial answers to their questions. Then there are also many who come who are already Christians, wanting to become more effective as God's people in the second half of the twentieth century. Many of these may already have heard Dr. Schaeffer during one of his visits to their country, as I did, or have heard of L'Abri through others, as for example did one student whilst staying in a youth hostel in Norway.

The word 'L'Abri' is the French word for 'shelter'. The desire is that all who go there, whether they are already Christians trying to find answers to the basic intellectual problems they face or not yet Christians looking for a meaning and purpose to life, may find for themselves a spiritual shelter.

On arriving for the first time, if you were more fortunate than I, who arrived in a torrential rain-storm, you would be captivated by the most beautiful scenery all around you. From almost any point in the village you can have an uninterrupted view down the Rhône valley towards the Mont Blanc range of mountains. On each side of the valley other mountains rise up several thousand feet forming a magnificent backdrop to the view. Of particular grandeur are the famous Dents du Midi to which the eye seems inevitably to return. As the sun moves round each day to set over the mountains bordering the Lake of Geneva, reflecting its crimson light on the snow-covered mountains, so the variations of colour on the trees and rocks keep changing. The combined effect of the scenery, reflecting something of the greatness and beauty of God, its personal creator, and the purpose for which L'Abri came into being seems to echo these words of Isaiah, 'Sing for joy, O heavens, and exult, O earth; break forth, O mountains, into singing! For the Lord has comforted his people, and will have compassion on his afflicted.'

Spread through the village are various chalets, all of which play their part in the work of the L'Abri Fellowship. The place where the work began is the Schaeffers' Chalet Les Mélèzes. The delightful chapel seemingly clutching the steep mountainside is a centre for worship and thanksgiving to God both in Sunday services and mid-week formal and not so formal concerts. The recently installed Flentrop organ plays a large part in the growing musical side in the work of L'Abri.

Though there are a number of other chalets which are used to house or entertain for meals the guests and students who stay, the increase in the numbers coming each year has strained the existing resources for accommodation. Needless to say, people who hope to make it merely a centre for a holiday are strongly discouraged. Those who come to L'Abri specifically to study are called 'Farel House students', after the first Swiss Reformer, who exerted considerable influence on that part of Switzerland.

The supremely important thing which underlies and undergirds all the activities, however seemingly trivial, is that those who make up the Christian family at L'Abri have stated as their purpose the desire 'To show forth, by demonstration in our life and work, the existence of God.'

They would all insist that to establish the reality of God's existence is not a matter of reasonable proof on the intellectual level alone, but a matter also of showing that the God 'who is there' is active in answer to specific prayer on the part of His own people. Prayer, therefore, is made to God about every aspect of the life of L'Abri.

In the twelve years since the L'Abri work started, the work has grown from one small family living in one chalet to a fair-sized family of workers, praying together and receiving people from all over the world into many chalets. There are further L'Abri workers in Milan, London, Amsterdam and America. Dr. Schaeffer is receiving many more requests to speak, from theological seminaries, university groups, colleges, churches and non-Christian groups, than he can possibly accept. The interest and eager longing to find reality in their lives on the part of so many whom a majority of evangelicals, at least, have written off as unreachable with the Christian Gospel, is a permanent source of wonder. No worker at L'Abri would want to do other than thank the one true God who alone has made all this possible by revealing to all who will listen the sufficient answer to their greatest longing.

This book is set forth as a statement of the urgent relevance of biblical Christianity to the gropings of many people who are shut up to the despair of twentieth-century thought. It is intended as an exposé of the bankruptcy of both secular and modern theological thought, but, far more than this, it gives a well-founded hope that man will again find his real personality and purpose if he will only turn to the life-giving Word which God has communicated in the record of Scripture.

As we read these pages, we must constantly remember that Christian apologetics should never become an end in itself. It is the great strength of Dr. Schaeffer's thought that it has not been produced from a study desk only, but from constant exposure to the doubts and perplexities of individual people from a great variety of backgrounds.

The purpose of this book would have been misconstrued if any reader took away from it merely ammunition to defend himself from the pressures of modern thought or to win intellectual arguments. If, however, it helps anyone to understand his own relationship with God better and also equips him to live out and communicate the Christian faith more realistically and effectively, then I know the author, and all who are associated with him in this work, will be profoundly grateful to the God who alone has brought it to pass.

Glossary of Terms Used in the Book

Agnostic: A person who does not know, or who thinks it is impossible to know, whether there is a God.

Atheist: A person who believes that there is no God.

Apologetics: That branch of theology having to do with the defence and communication of Christianity.

Antinomianism: Holding that, under the Gospel dispensation, the moral law is of no use or obligation.

Anti-philosophy: Many of the modern forms of philosophy which have given up any attempt to find a rational unity to the whole of thought and life.

Antithesis: Direct opposition of contrast between two things. (As in 'joy' which is the antithesis of 'sorrow'.)

Absolute: A concept which is not modifiable by factors such as culture, individual psychology or circumstances; but which is perfect and unchangeable. Used as an antithesis of relativism.

Archetype: The psychologist Jung interpreted dream symbols that have appeared throughout the history of man and called them archetypes.

Anthropology: That which deals only with man, his relationship with himself and with other men, such as the studies of psychology, and sociology, and nothing beyond man.

Authenticate oneself: A term used by existentialists whereby man validates the genuineness of his existence by an act of the will or a feeling of dread.

Being: A term denoting the area of bare existence.

Communication: The transmitting of ideas and information.

Connotation: The implication of meanings to words other than the definition of the word.

Cosmology: Theory of the nature and principles of the universe.

Dada: The name given to a modern art movement originating in Zürich in 1916. The name, chosen at random from a French dictionary, means 'rocking-horse'.

Determinism: The doctrine that human action is not free but results from such causes as psychological and chemical make-up which render free-will an illusion.

Dialectic: The principle of change which takes place by means of triadic movement. A thesis has its opposite, an antithesis. The two opposites are resolved in a synthesis which in turn becomes a thesis and the process goes on.

Dichotomy: Division into two totally separated parts. In this book used for the total separation of the rational and logical in man from both meaning and faith.

Epistemology: That part of philosophy concerned with the theory of knowledge, its nature, limits and validity.

Existential: Relating to and dealing with moment by moment human existence. Empirical reality as opposed to mere theory.

Existentialism: A modern theory of man that holds that human experience is not describable in scientific or rational terms. Existentialism stresses the need to make vital choices by using man's freedom in a contingent and apparently purposeless world.

Final Experience: Term used by Karl Jaspers to denote a crucial experience which is great enough to give hope of meaning.

Humanism: There are two meanings: (1) Any philosophy or system of thought that begins with man alone, in order to try to find a unified meaning to life; (2) That part of humanistic thinking in the above wider sense that stresses the hope of an optimistic future for mankind.

Impressionism: Movement in the visual arts in which the classical tendencies of nineteenth-century French painting culminated and from which modern art has sprung. Its aim was to reproduce, by means of a careful analysis of colour, the effect of light upon objects in nature.

Logic: The science of correct reasoning. The predictable and inevitable consequence of rational analysis. In classical logic it could be asserted that 'A' cannot equal 'non-A'.

Logical Positivism: Name given to an analytic trend in modern philosophy which holds that all metaphysical theories are strictly meaningless because, in the nature of the case, unverifiable by reference to empirical facts.

Linguistic Analysis: Branch of philosophy which desires to preserve philosophy from confusion of concepts by showing the use of these concepts in their natural language context. It sees the task of philosophy as clarifying what lies on the surface rather than offering explanations.

Mannishness of Man: Those aspects of man, such as significance, love, rationality and the fear of non-being, which mark him off from animals and machines and give evidence of his being created in the image of a personal God.

Methodology: Study of the procedures and principles whereby the question of truth and knowledge is approached.

Monolithic: Constituting one undifferentiated whole. In terms of modern culture, giving a unified message.

Mysticism: There are two meanings: (1) A tendency to seek direct communion with ultimate reality of 'the divine' by immediate intuition, insight or illumination; (2) A vague speculation without foundation.

Nihilism: A denial of all objective grounds for truth. A belief that existence is basically senseless and useless, leading often to destructive tendencies in society or in the individual.

Neo-orthodoxy: Name given to the theology of men who have particularly applied the dialectical methodology of Hegel and Kierkegaard's 'leap' to the Christian faith.

Pantheism: Doctrine that God and Nature are identical. The universe is an extension of God's essence rather than a special creation.

Presupposition: A belief or theory which is assumed before the next step in logic is developed. Such a prior postulate often consciously or unconsciously affects the way a person subsequently reasons.

Propositional Truth: Truth which can be communicated in the form of a statement in which a predicate or object is affirmed or denied regarding a subject.

Pragmatism: A system of thought which makes the practical consequences of a belief the sole test of truth.

Rational: Whatever is related to or based upon man's power to reason consistently.

Rationalism: cf. Humanism—first meaning.

Romantic: A view of life that has no base in fact, being the product of an exaggerated optimism.

Surrealism: An art-form which produces fantastic or incongruous imagery by means of unnatural juxta-positions and combinations, related to data plus the subconscious.

Semantics: (1) Science of the study of the development of the meaning and uses of words and language; (2) The exploitation of the connotations and ambiguities in words.

Substantial: A term used to denote the extent of healing in the relationships of man with God, with his fellow man and within himself which should be seen in the life of a Christian—not perfect and yet visible in reality.

Synthesis: The combination of the partial truths of a thesis and its antithesis into a higher stage of truth, cf. dialectic.

'*Upper Storey*': Term used to denote that which, in modern thinking, deals with significance or meaning, but which is not open to contact with verification by the world of facts which constitute the 'Lower storey'.

Validity: Something which has been authenticated by reference to well-grounded and sufficient evidence.

Verbalisation: The putting of a proposition into words.

Verification: The procedure required for the establishment of the truth or falsity of a statement.

Notes

SECTION I

Chapter 1

[1] The consideration of classical and presuppositional apologetics is continued in section IV, Chapter 2, p. 126 ff.
[2] Allen and Unwin, London, 1961.
[3] James 1 : 27.

Chapter 2

[1] This book is not intended to be exhaustive in its treatment of the developments from the time of the Renaissance leading up to Hegel. Another book of mine, *Escape from Reason*, gives a more complete résumé of the developments from Aquinas, through the Renaissance, the birth of modern science, and including the place of Kant.
[2] Cf., e.g. Professor A. J. Ayer in *What I Believe* ed. by Unwin (Allen and Unwin, London, 1966), and *Must Morality Pay?* by Professor Anthony Flew in *The Listener*, October 13, 1966.
[3] *The Humanist Frame* ed. by Sir Julian Huxley, p. 46.
[4] ibid, p. 409.
[5] University Books, New York, 1964.

Chapter 3

[1] See pp. 56, 60.
[2] This is the translation suggested by Dr. H. R. Rookmaaker in *Synthetist Art Theories* (Amsterdam, 1959), p. 23 and note W to Chapter IX.
[3] A letter written in February 1898.
[4] Dr. Rookmaaker, *op. cit.* notes n, p, aa, af to chapter 9.
[5] Two works with Eva's name written on them were exhibited in the Picasso and Man Exhibition at the Toronto Art Gallery, January 1964.
[6] *FÜR THEO van Doesburg*, DE STIJL, January 1932.

Chapter 4

[1] See paragraph on the Beatles, pp. 42-43.
[2] Ducretet-Thomson, Paris, no. 320 c. 100.

³ *Collected Poems, 1934–52* (J. M. Dent and Sons, London, 1959), pp. 179–80.
⁴ S.M.O. Records, 81.045.
⁵ E.M.I. Records, R5570.
⁶ E.M.I. Records, P.M.C. 7027.

Chapter 5

¹ Frederick A. Praeger, New York, 1964.
² *Selected Poems* by Léopold Sédar Senghor (Oxford University Press, 1964).
³ French Jesuit paleontologist who wrote *The Phenomenon of Man* (Collins, London, 1959) and other books.
⁴ Sir Julian Huxley wrote the Introduction to the British edition of *The Phenomenon of Man* in 1958. In this he agrees both with the methodology and broad conclusions of Teilhard de Chardin regarding the evolutionary future of man. Later, in 1961, he develops his general agreement with these conclusions in the direction of the use of religion in his Introduction to *The Humanist Frame*. What Senghor does in his book in applying Teilhard de Chardin's principles to the State of Senegal, Huxley seeks to do on a global scale.
⁵ Cf. I Corinthians 15:13–14, 32.

SECTION II

Chapter 2

¹ My thinking has led me to believe that there is a collective cultural consciousness or memory which is related to words. I would suggest there are two parts to it: a collective memory of a specific race, and a collective memory of all men as to what man is and what reality is.

Thus man, in his *language*, 'remembers' (regardless of his personal belief) that God does exist. For example, when the Russian leaders curse, they curse by God, and not by something less; and atheistic artists often use 'god' symbols. This, I believe, is a deeper yet simpler explanation than Jung's view of god as the supreme archetype arising (according to him) out of the evolution of the race. Moreover, in man's language, man also remembers that humanity is unique (created in the image of God) and therefore words like purpose, love, morals, carry with them in connotation their real meaning. This is the case regardless of the individual's personal world-view and despite what the dictionary or scientific textbook definition has become.

At times the connotation of the word is deeper and more 'unconscious' than its definition. The use of such words trigger responses to a greater degree in line with what the specific race has thought they mean and how it has acted on their meaning, and to a lesser degree in line with

what really is and what man is. I would further suggest that, after the
world-view and experiences of the race form the definition and connotation of the words of any specific language, then that language as a
symbol system becomes the vehicle for keeping alive and teaching this
world-view and experience.

It would therefore seem to me that the whole matter is primarily one of
language, as man thinks and communicates in language. I would say
that in this context the division of languages at the tower of Babel is
an overwhelmingly profound moment of history.

[2] *Leonardo da Vinci* (Raynal and Company, New York, 1956), p. 174.

[3] I am consciously omitting here the intermediate and important
change in the formulation at the time of Kant (1724–1804) and Rousseau
(1712–78). That formulation was:

$$\frac{\text{Freedom}}{\text{Nature}}$$

[4] Cf. the attitude of the Bereans to Paul's teaching, Acts 17:11–12.

Chapter 3

[1] *Berenson*, A Biography, by Sylvia Sprigge (Houghton Mifflin, 1960).
[2] Cf. 1 Corinthians 15:6.
[3] Published in 1920.
[4] In the same way you have a parallel situation with the two women
Picasso married. One is a very human picture of Olga, painted in
1917–18, the other is a lovely painting of Jacqueline done on October
5, 1954. There is a further parallel in that Jacqueline keeps this drawing
in her sitting room. In all three of these paintings it is not only that the
painting speaks of the love of the artist for his wife, but the woman has
meaning as a human being.
[5] Since his painting of the *Basket of Bread*, he has painted many
pictures in which a Mary-like figure is the focus-point of the painting.
The Gallery of Modern Art in New York has some of these paintings
in which the figure appears several times in one painting. However, on
inspection, one sees that these Mary-like figures are portraits of Dali's
wife.
[6] Vision Press Ltd., London, 1956.

Chapter 4

[1] Columbia KL 6005 or KS 6005.
[2] November 28, 1964, by Calvin Tomkins.
[3] Because his theories have produced in music noise or total silence,
which is therefore monotonous, most modern music has not followed
him. But through Merce Cunningham and others, John Cage has

become the central force in modern dance against Martha Graham who put much emphasis on form and meaning.

[4] The translation of this preface is that which appeared in *Vogue*, December 1964.

[5] The preceding context identifies this as the dropping of the bomb.

Chapter 5

[1] In recent years it is often said that Karl Barth has changed his views. If this is so then all could be easily cared for by his writing one more book amongst his many books and, while he is yet living, making it known that his views of Scripture, his lack of a space-time Fall and his implicit universalism have been publicly repudiated. In the light of his crucial influence as the originator of the new theology and his wide publication, it would seem difficult to think that anything less could meet his responsibility before God and men. If he did this many of us would truly rejoice. Note pp. 102, 103 for a consideration of the deficient concept of justification and the place of universalism in the new theology.

[2] The italics are mine.

[3] As an example see *When is a word an event?* by Dr. Alan Richardson in *The Listener*, June 3, 1965.

[4] *The Unknown Christ of Hinduism* (Darton, Longman and Todd, London, 1964).

[5] *Jubilee*, November 1963.

[6] Loyola University ecumenical forum as reported in the Chicago *Daily News-Post Dispatch*, December 14, 1963.

SECTION III

Chapter 1

[1] In John 17:24 Jesus, in His prayer to His Father, speaks of the love with which 'Thou lovedst me before the foundation of the world'. In Genesis 1:26 there is reported communication within the Trinity.

[2] *The Wild Duck.*

Chapter 2

[1] Constable and Co. Ltd., London, pp. 90–91.

[2] Exodus 24:12.

[3] Acts 26:14.

[4] John 17:24.

Chapter 3

[1] Translated from the French by Stuart Gilbert (Penguin Books in association with Hamish Hamilton, 1966), *La Peste*, 1947.
[2] The consideration of *The Plague* is continued on pp. 106-107.
[3] John 5:24; Colossians 1:13.
[4] Genesis 2:17.
[5] It is intriguing that the new Heidegger, as he changed his position, tried to get a historic Fall into his new system. He says there was a Golden Age (before this Fall) at the time of the pre-Socratic Greeks; and then Aristotle, and those who followed him, fell. Their fall was that they began to think rationally. So Heidegger is now saying that man is abnormal. There is no historical evidence for such a Golden Age, but it does indicate that the usual rationalistic answer to man's dilemma, which says man is as he has always been, is insufficient. In Heidegger's desperate theory, Aristotle takes the place of Adam, as the one who fell, and it does appear as if Heidegger sees himself as the one who will save. But notice that his concept of the Fall and salvation does not touch moral issues. Man's abnormality is not moral; in Heidegger's new system it is rather epistemological and methodological abnormality. Aristotle was not morally wrong in what he did, according to Heidegger; he was just introducing the faulty methodology of antithesis and rationality. There is no answer here for man's dilemma, but Heidegger has clearly shown that philosophy has no answer to man's dilemma on the basis of man and history now being normal. It would seem that Heidegger would like Christianity's answer, but without bowing to God—either morally or in acknowledging the need of knowledge from Him.

Chapter 4

[1] Cf. p. 101.
[2] Simone de Beauvoir deals with the same problem in a slightly different setting in her book *A Very Easy Death* (Putnam, 1966).
[3] See *Biblical and Theological Studies* by B. B. Warfield (Scribners' Sons, New York, 1912), *On the emotional life of our Lord*, pp. 35-90.

Chapter 5

[1] 'As the arch-revolutionary, Einstein says: "The historical development has shown that among the imaginable theoretical constructions there is invariably one that proves to be unquestionably superior to all others. Nobody who really goes into the matter will deny that the world of perceptions determines the theoretical system in a virtually unambiguous manner." A man engaged in solving a well designed word-puzzle may, it is true, propose any word as the solution but there

is only *one* word which really solves the puzzle in all its forms. It is an outcome of faith that nature takes the character of such a well formulated puzzle. The successes reaped up to now by science do, it is true, give a certain encouragement for this faith.' *Scientific Theories* by H. R. Post in *The Listener*, February 10, 1966.

[2] Romans 1:18–20, R.V.

[3] In an article in *The Christian Century* of May 12, 1965, entitled *The Modernity of Fundamentalism*, John Opie Jr. makes two main mistakes. He says correctly that historic Christianity (which he calls fundamentalism) is primarily separated from the new theology not in theological detail, but in epistemology and methodology, because it insists on rationality. However, he then goes on to say that historic Christianity is interested *exclusively* in rationality. This is not so. The other mistake he makes, a foolish one, is his saying that the kind of thinking upon which historic Christianity is based, that is, rational thinking, began with the enlightenment. This view has no more support than Heidegger's when he says that it began with Aristotle, and is even more impossible to support. Other men in the new theology make this same mistake. For example, Ernest R. Sandeen in his article *The Princeton Theology* in *Church History*, September 1962.

[4] 1 John 4:1–3, R.V.

SECTION IV

Chapter 1

[1] Acts 17:26.
[2] Psalm 139:8.
[3] Romans 1:32–2:3.

Chapter 2

[1] See section I, p. 15.
[2] The basic concepts presented here were put forth first in my article entitled *A Review of a Review* in *The Bible Today*, vol. 42, No. 1, October 1948.

Romans 1:18 reads: 'For the wrath of God is revealed from heaven against all ungodliness and unrighteousness of men, who hold the truth in unrighteousness.' The context shows that this 'holding the truth in unrighteousness' is related to the 'general revelation' of the 'mannishness' of man and the external universe in verses 19 and 20. The concept involved in the phrase 'who hold the truth in unrighteousness' has two possibilities: in many of the newer translations it is translated as *hinder*, *hold down*, *stifle*, *restrain* or *suppress* the truth—which men have from the general revelation of the external creation and man's 'mannishness'. Probably a more accurate meaning, from the Greek word used, is that they *hold* that portion of the truth of the real world that they must hold (in spite of their non-Christian presuppositions) but, because of their unrighteousness, their rebellion, they do not carry the logic of the general revelation to its natural and proper conclusion. Thus they are, in the strict sense, without excuse.

Chapter 3

[1] Hebrews 11:6.
[2] Acts 16:30–32.
[3] Bunyan's note at this place is: 'Come unto me, all ye that labour and are heavy laden, and I will give you rest.' Matthew 11:28.
[4] The ninth stage of *Pilgrim's Progress*.
[5] The following references in the Bible will help anyone who wants to read more about becoming a Christian: John 3:15–18, Romans 3:9–26, Romans 4:1–3, Galatians 2:16, Galatians 3:24, John 8:24, John 14:6, Acts 4:12. Romans chapters 1–8 is a good section in which to see the unity of becoming a Christian and what follows after one is a Christian.

SECTION V

Chapter 1

[1] John 20:30, 31.
[2] Luke 1:1–4.

Chapter 2

[1] Mark 12:30; Deuteronomy 6:5.

SECTION VI

Chapter 1

[1] John 17:21.
[2] Matthew 5:48.
[3] 1 John 2:1.
[4] Romans 7:22–25.
[5] 2 Corinthians 13:14.

Index

Algerian Manifesto, 56, 124
American 'Black Writers', 72
Anti-Law, 38
Anti-Statement Novel, 42
Antonioni, Michelangelo, 42
Appel, Karel, 90
Aristotle, 60, 68, 185, 186
Armory Show, The, 35, 53, 54
Arp, Hans, 34
Art Zero, 35
Aquinas, Thomas, 60
Ascherson, Neal, 83
Ayer, A. J., 181

Bach, Johann Sebastian, 58
Barth, Karl, 22, 52, 54, 80, 184
Baudelaire, Charles, 100, 101
Beatles, The, 42, 43
Berenson, Barnard, 64, 65
Bergman, Ingmar, 42
Bernstein, Leonard, 70
Bezzant, J. S., 93
Bocaccio, Giovanni, 60
Bonhoeffer, Dietrich, 79
Bornkamm, Gunther, 81
Boston Museum of Art, 31
Boulez, Pierre, 71
Bultmann, Rudolph, 51, 81, 94
Bunyan, John, 135

Cage, John, 43, 70–74, 90, 91, 109, 126, 183
Calvin, John, 59
Camus, Albert, 24, 56, 101, 107, 123, 124
Capote, Truman, 42
Cézanne, Paul, 30, 32
Cimabue, 60
Communism, 45
Costelloe, Mary, 64

Crick, Francis, 103
Cubism, 32
Cunningham, Merce, 183

Dada, 34, 35, 66
Dali, Salvador, 65–68, 75, 77, 100, 160
Dante, Alighieri, 60
Da Vinci, Leonardo, 30, 59, 60
De Beauvoir, Simone, 185
Debussy, Claude, 37
Defining Philosophy, 22, 24–26
De Mello, Anthony, 83
De Stijl, 34
Duchamp, Marcel, 35

Einstein, Albert, 57, 63, 185
Engels, Friedrich, 45
Environments, 34, 35

Favre, Elie, 74, 75
Feldman, Morty, 72
Fellini, Frederico, 41
Ficino, Marsilio, 60
Flew, Anthony, 181
Francis I, King of France, 59
Freud, Sigmund, 66

Garaudy, Roger, 84
Gauguin, Paul, 30, 31, 55
Gentile, Giovanni, 59
Giotto, di Bondone, 60, 66
Glasgow Art Gallery, 66
Graham, Martha, 184
Greeks, The, 94
Green, Michael, 94
Griffiths, Dom Bede, 83

Happenings, 34–36
Hegel, Georg Wilhelm, 20, 21, 44, 45, 52

Heidegger, Martin, 22, 24, 68, 69, 82, 185, 186
Henry, Pierre, 38
High Fidelity Magazine, 70
Hinduism, 45, 83, 101
Hodge, Charles, 114
Homosexuality, Philosophic, 39
Huxley, Aldous, 27
Huxley, Julian, 16, 26, 79, 83, 88, 182

Ibsen, Henrik, 89
Impressionists, 30
Indo-European Culture, 18

Jaspers, Karl, 22, 23
Jazz, 37
Jung, Carl Gustav, 57, 122

Kant, Emmanuel, 21, 26, 183
Kierkegaard, Søren, 21, 22, 44, 51, 54, 60
Klee, Paul, 65, 66, 69, 71
Küng, Hans, 83

Last Year in Marienbad, 55, 84
Leary, Timothy, 27
Listeners, The BBC, 29, 81, 181, 184, 186
Logical Positivism, 24, 25
Luther, Martin, 18, 39, 132

Mace, Thomas, 72
Macquarrie, John, 81, 82
Marcis, Leonard, 70
Marx, Karl, 45
Mass Media, 41, 42
Mathieu, Georges, 71
McLuhan, Marshall, 43
Miller, Henry, 38, 39, 74–77, 80
Mondrian, 33, 34
Museum of Modern Art, New York, 32, 183
Musique Concrète, 37, 38, 44, 55, 58

National Gallery of Art, Washington, 67

Neo-Orthodoxy, 51, 52, 53, 56
New Yorker, 70–74
Niebuhr, Reinhold, 54

Op Art, 38
Opie, John, 186
Osborne, John, 39

Panikkar, Raymond, 83
Pantheism, 57, 66, 67, 74, 76, 79, 88, 90
Paul, The Apostle, 65, 96, 106, 111, 123, 133, 134, 155, 156, 183
Paulus Society, 83
Petrarch, 60
Philadelphia Museum of Art, 35
Picasso, Pablo, 32, 33, 60, 66, 67, 122, 183
Plaque, The, 101, 106, 107, 124
Planck, Max, 67, 145
Pollock, Jackson, 71
Post, H. R., 186
Provos, Amsterdam, 36

Rahner, Karl, 83, 84
Reformation, The, 51, 52, 53, 59
Renaissance, The, 33, 59, 60, 64, 70
Renoir, Pierre Auguste, 32
Richardson, Alan, 54, 184
Rietveld, 33
Robinson, John A. T., 54
Rookmaaker, Hans, 181
Russell, Bertrand, 111
Russia, 83
Rutherford, 114

Sade, Marquis de, 39, 103
Sandeen, Ernest, 186
Sartre, Jean Paul, 22–24, 56, 123, 124
Schaeffer, Pierre, 37, 38, 58
Schweitzer, Albert, 95
Senegal, 44, 45
Senghor, Leopold Sedar, 44, 45, 51, 83
Shute, Nevil, 76
Silas, 133, 134

Slessinger, 42
Stadelijk Museum, Amsterdam, 33, 35, 36
Stein, Gertrude, 32
Surrealism, 66
Susiki, Daisetz, 71
Synthetist Art Theories, 181

Teilhard de Chardin, Pierre, 45, 67, 83, 88, 182
Thomas, Dylan, 40, 41, 46
Tibetan Book of the Dead, 27
Tillich, Paul, 54, 58, 79, 88
Times, The, 36

Tomkins, Calvin, 183
Toronto Art Gallery, 181
Turner, Joseph, 30

Unknown Christ of Hinduism, 184

Van der Leck, 33
Vogue Magazine, 184

Warfield, Benjamin B., 185
Weinrib, David, 73
Whitman, Walt., 74, 75

Zen Buddhism, 71, 103